Ecclesiology of Prophetic Participation

Ecclesiology of Prophetic Participation

Viju Wilson

South Asia Leadership Training and
Development Centre (SALT DC)

2012

Ecclesiology of Prophetic Participation — Jointly published by the Rev. Dr. Ashish Amos of the Indian Society for Promoting Christian Knowledge (ISPCK), Post Box 1585, 1654, Madarsa Road, Kashmere Gate, Delhi-110006 and South Asia Leadership Training and Development Centre (SALT DC), Pipariya, Hoshangabad, Madhya Pradesh.

© Author, 2012

All rights reserved. No part of this book may be reproduced or transmitted in any form or by any means, electronic, mechanical, photocopying, recording, or by any information storage and retrieval system, without the prior permission in writing from the publisher.

The views expressed in the book are those of the author and the publishers take no responsibility for any of the statements.

Ecclesiology of Prophetic Participation is revised version of the selected sections of the theses submitted to the Senate of Serampore College in partial fulfilment of the requirement for the degrees of Bachelor of Divinity (B.D.) and Master of Theology (M.Th.) in 2005 and 2008 respectively

ISBN: 978-81-8465-214-7

Laser typeset by

ISPCK, Post Box 1585, 1654, Madarsa Road, Kashmere Gate, Delhi-110006 • *Tel:* 23866323/22

e-mail: ashish@ispck.org.in • ella@ispck.org.in
website: www.ispck.org.in

Dedication

This book is dedicated to
Dr. P. G. Vargis,
Founder President of Indian Evangelical
Team and South Asia Leadership Training and
Development Centre
in recognition of his innumerable contribution
towards Christian ministry.

CONTENTS

Dedication v

Acknowledgements ix

Introduction xi

Chapter 1

Situating the Church in the Indian Context   1

Chapter 2

The Ecclesiology of Dietrich Bonhoeffer   17

Chapter 3

Church as New Humanity in Christ: The Ecclesiology of M. M. Thomas   38

Chapter 4

Church as New Humanity in Christ: An Intentional Engagement with People   76

Chapter 5

The Theology of Paulose Mar Paulose   105

Chapter 6

The Ecclesiology of Paulose Mar Paulose   130

Chapter 7

The Political Witness of the Church in India:
A Theological Appraisal   143

Chapter 8

Political Witness: A Journey of Affirming Life   152

Conclusion   160

Bibliography   168

Acknowledgements

I express my sincere gratitude to my thesis mentors, Rev. Dr. Mathew C. Varghese and Dr. George Zachariah, for their valuable guidance and resourceful insights. I am extremely grateful to Dr. P. G. Vargis, the Founder of South Asia Leadership Training and Development Centre (SALT DC) for giving prayer support and for rendering financial assistance in getting this book published. I am also thankful to IET Theological Council for granting permission to bring out this work on behalf of SALT DC. I am greatly indebted to Rev. V. D. John, Principal, SALT DC, for his encouragement and for the initiative he took in getting approval and financial support from the authorities at IET and SALT DC. Thanks are due to the ISPCK family, Delhi, for publishing this book.

Viju Wilson

SALT DC, Jhiriya

Pipariya, Hoshangabad

M.P.

Introduction

The vocation of the Church cannot be limited to the religious realm alone: it embraces all spheres of community life. However, it has been observed that the Church in India, in general, is a communal organisation that strives to safeguard its own rights and privileges. In the Indian context, the Church does not witness as light and salt. In this tragic predicament of the Indian Church, the nature and witness of the Church needs to be re-defined in the light of the Gospel and contemporary societal challenges.

The Indian Church is located in a pluralistic context of varied human experiences and identities. It is sad to note that the faith communities in India have failed miserably in responding adequately to the struggles of the people. Instead of standing with the people in establishing their rights and privileges, the Church gives priority to its vested interests and communal politics. It does not mean that the Church should not stand for its rights. But the Church is currently involved in the political process mainly to defend minority rights and to accomplish its vested interests. The Indian Church is much concerned about safeguarding minority rights to protect minority institutions. It opposes those policies of the government that are against the interests of the Christian community; but remains silent when the oppressed communities are deprived of equal rights and dignity. If there is any bill or law or Government programme or scheme that affects the minority rights, the community unites in the name of faith and opposes it tooth and nail. The Church even misuses minority rights by forgetting the social commitment behind those rights. The disturbing question before us is, Are we able to make use of minority rights to empower the weaker sections of the society? Problems within the Church often keep it away from involving in the realities of society. In this context, the vocation of the Church and its political witness in India must be understood freshly. Its political witness must be responsive to the issues of wider human community.

The Christian community, irrespective of denominations, expresses its anxiety and pain when it is targeted and misrepresented. But the question is how often the faith community expressed its strong protest and grief when the people of other minority communities and subaltern groups were persecuted in the Indian society? It is also a fact that the real spirit of Christian ecumenism is evident in society when the Christian community is embattled.

The vocation of the Church in India becomes theologically valid if it addresses the vital issues of society, because involvement in human struggles is the prophetic vision of Jesus. It must call the people to work for the elimination of economic and social injustice. It should support the Government for the programmes that are aimed to help those who are under unjust structures of society. The Church must consider the plight of the poor farmers in the country, reject communal politics and raise voice for those who have lost their land because of development projects. Instead of arguing for sectarian interests, the influence of the Church must be used to engage with actual life situation and to participate in the movements of protest. The Church should join hands with secular movements to work for human development.

It is sad to note that today's ecclesiastical bodies are not being motivated to raise voice for the rights of underprivileged classes. But the Christian community has a history of struggling to protect communal interests. Today, the Church is situated in a communally polarised social context. Therefore, it is the need of the hour to consider again the witness of the Church, especially the political witness, in the context of the struggles, hopes and aspirations of the people.

The ecclesiology of Dietrich Bonhoeffer, M. M. Thomas and Paulose Mar Paulose gives the guideline for formulating a praxis-oriented faith-response of the Church to the broken human realties.

Chapter 1

Situating the Church in the Indian Context

The pluralistic context of India is characterised by diverse ethnic-linguistic-cultural identities and multi-religious traditions. Plurality recognises the validity of varied human experiences, belief systems and cultural practices. At the same time, it is an undeniable fact that the Indian pluralist setting is more religiously sensitive and religion plays a very significant role in all aspects of community life. Often the people of pluralist heritage are mobilised more on the basis of caste, religion, language and ethnicity for the vested interests of communal identity than the well-being of the entire society. Today, the forces of disintegration, such as religious fundamentalism, communalism, parochialism, criminalisation of politics and fascist-communal ideologies pose division among the people. Diverse identities are manipulated to legitimise dominant socio-economic and political interests. Politicised religion and communalised politics jeopardise the secular ethos and democratic values. The majority and minority forms of communalism equally create social unrest, separatism and violence between religious communities. The faith communities of India often tempt to be communal organisations that are politically irresponsive, neutral on the pertinent issues of poor people and aversive to secular movements.

Social Milieu

The social context of India is characterised by the caste system, patriarchy, etc. The caste factor in its varied forms plays an important role in all aspects of social life. The hierarchical and oppressive nature of the caste system marginalises and excludes many low-caste people in the mainstream of society. The caste factor is attributed divine mandate and works on the basis of purity-pollution norms and unjust regulations. According to Felix Wilfred, "modernity with all its IT revolution and with high profile entrepreneurial and managerial mantras has not changed an iota in the frame of mind that is soaked in caste consciousness."[1] Dalits are the most affected people in Indian society due to the stigma of caste consciousness. They are denied human dignity and face discrimination in all walks of life.[2] In spite of the economic,

---

[1] Felix Wilfred, "Subalterns and Ethical Auditing," *Jeevadhara* Vol. XXXVII/ No.217 (January 2007): 7.

[2] Because of untouchability, the very nature of caste system, Dalits are segregated in public places such as schools, hospitals, shops, tea stalls and public wells or taps. Due to the lack of quality education and finance, Dalits do not get employment opportunities. A vast majority of Dalits in village locations are deprived of their right to vote, right to stand for election and right to be elected. Dalit villages are overlooked by government agencies for development. Wherever they raise voice for justice, they face large-scale violence, destruction of their property and sexual violence against their woman. Rf. Jimmy Dabhi, "Dalit Human Rights: Issues and Perspective," *Social Action* Vol. 24/No.1 (January- March, 2004): 34, 36, 38 & 42. Their struggles continue even today.

educational and technological development, the intensity of casteism in the 21st century Indian society can be evident in the anti-reservation agitations in All India Institute of Medical Sciences (AIIMS), New Delhi, and in the Sukhadeo Thorat Committee Report on AIIMS.[3] Like the caste system, under patriarchal structure, women are discriminated at different levels.[4]

---

[3] The anti-reservation protests were held under the banner of Youth for Equality that argues for the merit-oriented admission of students against quota and reservation systems. The Sukhadeo Thorat committee report reveals that due to harassment from upper-caste student groups, Dalit and Tribal students moved out of their hostel rooms to live in clusters among themselves. They face social isolation, refusal to share books and notes and objections to sharing seats in the classrooms. They find it difficult to access the private messes. Their low-caste identity leads to low participation in the cultural events of the Institute. Every aspect of academic life becomes miserable for the low-caste students. Rf.Editorial, "Sukhdeo Thorat Committee Report: Caste Discrimination in AIIMS," *Economic and Political Weekly* Vol. XLII/No.22 (June 2-8, 2007): 2032.

[4] The patriarchal culture restricts women the access to education, property and other social privileges. It creates division of labour on gender basis and uses all kinds of social pressures including violence to maintain the status quo, especially the oppressive condition of the woman. Under patriarchy, women experience discrimination in the family, employment, etc. They face violence—communal and caste, dowry death and sexual and commercial exploitation. Among them, Dalit-Tribal women are thrice oppressed. As women, they undergo patriarchal restrictions, caste stigma keeps them away from the mainstream of the society and economically they are not empowered due to economic exploitation and unemployment. Rf.Gabriele Dietrich and Bas Wielenga, *Towards Understanding Indian Society* (Madurai: TTS, 1997), 37. & John Desrochers, *The Social Teaching of the Church in India* (Bangalore: NBCLC/CSA, 2006), 37.

Here it can be argued that caste[5] and patriarchy[6] are still the main issues in Indian social setting that affect the life of the subaltern people. Therefore, their voices for equal rights and privileges are seldom heard in society. It is interesting to note that the Indian Church is also not free from the bondage of caste and patriarchy.

Political Condition

The Indian political scenario is plural in nature. National and regional parties lead the central and state governments with their political agendas. Though the political movements are based on their respective ideologies, often money, religion, caste and regionalism play a vital role on the way to attain power. Today, people have lost their expectation of minimum justice and protection of rights from the authorities. Very often, the voters have no political-ideological choice than communal-regional priorities. Parliamentary democracy is under the threat of corruption, money-power and gun-culture. Instead of socialist politics, communal politics dominate the political situation of our secular state.[7] Polarised politics based on religion and caste and other ethnic identities destroy the moral values of secular politics. The so-called people's governments that pretend to be the protectors of the rights of poor marginalised groups neglect the legitimate demands of poor people and support the vested interests of the rich and the

---

[5] Human Rights Watch, *Broken People, Caste Violence Against India's "Untouchables"* (New York: Human Rights Watch, 1999) & Ninan Koshy, *Caste in the Kerala Churches* (Bangalore: CISRS, 1968).

[6] Amruta Rao, *Sex Discrimination* (Delhi: Indian Publishers Distributors, 2000) and Kamla Bhasin, *What is Patriarchy?* (New Delhi: Kali for Women, 1993).

[7] Dietrich and Wielenga, *Towards Understanding Indian Society*, 145 & 176.

powerful.⁸ The unholy nexus between politics and religious fundamentalism breeds fascism, criminalisation of politics and communalised politics.⁹ The communal politics perpetuates communal violence. Women, children, Dalits and Tribals are the worst affected by communal violence.¹⁰ The best examples of communalised politics are the communal riots of Gujarat in 2002 and the Kandhamal violence in Orissa in 2008.

Patriarchal dominance is an important feature of the Indian political scenario. The patriarchal supremacy that ignores gender equality guaranteed in the constitution can be seen in the delay of passing the Women's Reservation Bill, which provides 33 per cent reservation for women in the Parliament and Legislative assemblies. Though there is reservation at the panchayat level, women face pressure tactics, non-corporation, character assassination, etc.¹¹ Communalised

---

⁸ John Desrochers, *Towards a New India* (Bangalore: CSA, 1995), 91.

⁹ The greatest threat to Indian secularism is the communalisation of politics. Political parties use the religious card to get votes and to keep the power intact. Here religion is used to mobilise people to protect the vested interests of politicians. Communal violence is a part of this political strategy. Rf.Descrochers, *The Social Teaching of the Church in India*, 40.

¹⁰ It is an undeniable fact that minority community members are detained largely under the laws of POTA, TADA, etc., as part of political vengeance by communal politicians. It is also to be noted that communalism pushes down humanitarian ideals and upholds ideas of ethnic cleansing. The Hindu fascist political forces make use of religion to come to power. The communal upsurge among the Muslims appears as a reaction to Hindutva politics. The communalism promoted by politicians is in touch with 'Brahminic' religious orthodoxy. Rf. Lancy Lobo, "Communalism and Christian Response in India," *Vidyajyoti Journal of Theological Reflections* Vol.LIX/No.6 (June, 1995): 367.

¹¹ Patriarchy literally prevents women from political life though there are some exceptional cases. The political rights of women are not properly raised by male politicians. Their life realities are not

politics creates a communally polarised society and patriarchal power keeps women away from the mainstream of politics. The Christian community is also becoming part of communal politics by standing more for minority rights and by supporting the political parties that stand for their vested interests than for wider issues.

Economic Scenario

Indian economy is considered as one of the growing economies in the world. A majority of Indians live in rural areas. Most of them are agricultural workers. They live below the poverty line. They work in the unorganised sector.[12] Though economists show the acceleration of economic growth, many farmers have committed suicide and hunger, disease and poverty are prevalent all over the country. The liberalisation reforms do not benefit the common people and the environment. There is a wide gap between the rich and the poor and the urban and rural areas in development. Rural poverty brings several problems of large-scale migration and urbanisation. Due to lack of state attention to rural areas, public services, such as health care and education, have collapsed. Children die of malnutrition. Though child labour is abolished, a large number of children are in the labour market.[13] Poverty[14] is a common phenomenon in society.

---

becoming the topics of discussion in the conferences and meetings of political parties. Rf. T.A. John, "Gender Equality: Chasing a Millennium Goal for the Long Haul," *Social Action* Vol. 57/No.2 (April -June, 2007): 161-162.

[12] Dietrich and Wielenga, *Towards Understanding Indian Society*, 112.

[13] Simon Paul D'souza, "India At Sixty" *Integral Liberation* Vol. 2/No.3 (September, 2007): 176-178.

[14] It is estimated that one in every five Indians suffers from overt or covert hunger. 300 millions of Indians are still surviving with less than a dollar a day. Though government claims that poverty rates are falling, it is only above 1 per cent per year. Poverty hits mostly Dalits,

Dalits[15] are the most vulnerable section in the labour sector. Tribals[16] have been badly hit by industrial and infrastructural projects. In India, globalisation[17] helps the rich and brings

---

Adivasis and other economically backward communities, among them women suffer a lot. Rf. Y. Moses, "Peoples' Politics and the Role of the Indian Church," *NCC Review* Vol. CXXVI/No.10 (November, 2006): 50.

[15] In the unorganised sector, many workers are Dalits. Most of the bonded labourers in India come from SC/ST communities. It is also suggested that child labourers are largely from SC/ST families; a majority of them are girls. They are not paid the minimum wage and subject to child abuse. Poverty and related issues in livelihood compel many Dalit girls and women to be sex workers. Their life situation is not highlighted in the developmental policies. Though there are various empowerment programmes for these people, they are not benefited because of the apathy of government officials. Rf. Jimmy Dahbi, "Dalit Human Rights, Issues and Perspective," 39-40.

[16] Tribals are displaced from their land and homes due to the developmental projects. It directly takes away their support system for livelihood. Displacement destroys the existing socio-cultural fabric and economic base of tribal families. It reduces employment opportunities and gradually leads them into impoverishment. It affects their pattern of social organisation and interpersonal ties. In fact, the Tribals become landless, jobless and homeless and suffer from food insecurity, loss of access to common property, loss of access to community services, loss of educational opportunities. Rf. Sarbeswar Sahoo, "Tribal Displacement and Human Rights Violations in Orissa," *Social Action* Vol. 55/No. 2 (April -June, 2005): 160-163.

[17] The arrival of multinational companies causes the declination of local industries and the price reduction of the products of poor farmers. The promotion of commercial tourism and developmental projects results in the displacement of poor people and diverts basic infrastructures like water supply, electricity, etc., for the globalised Indian and foreign multinational companies. Privatisation of public property deprives the poor of their basic requirements of fodder, fuel and water. New technologies make the traditional artisans, craftsmen and weavers jobless. Women are exploited in the labour market and are being paid lower wages than men for the same work. Though globalisation brought few benefits, the aggressive competitive market

heavy burden on the poor. Because of the privatisation policy in the public sector, the Dalits lose their reservation privilege. Since Dalits do not get quality education, they are not able to enjoy the benefits of globalisation. Under globalisation, quality education is limited to the wealthy and poor Dalits suffer for their daily livelihood.[18] Special Economic Zones, another expression of globalisation, put the life of farmers and poor rural people under tension and chaos.[19] The above analysis

---

economy seldom realises the basic rights of poor marginalised labourers and agricultural workers who struggle for their livelihood. Rf. Desrochers, "The Social Teaching of the Church in India," 38-39.

[18] James Massey, "An Analysis of the Dalit situation with Special Reference to Dalit Christians and Dalit Theology," *Religion and Society* Vol. 52/No. 3-4 (September-December, 2007): 69-70.

[19] Since Special Economic Zones need a large amount of land, the state governments acquire the land of farmers with the promise of employment opportunities and rehabilitation. It causes large-scale displacement of people. Though Special Economic Zones promise employment opportunities, they do not keep the promise. They not only take away the jobs of agricultural labourers, but also reduce food grains. It is also important to note that these zones are mostly established in agricultural lands where poor people are employed. They get a meagre amount as compensation and become jobless and homeless. But people who are under the threat of land acquisition for Special Economic Zones started to fight against the establishment of such globalised exploitative zones. Now the people are aware of their rights on land and of the pro-capitalist stand of respective governments. The protest of indigenous people has become violent in many parts of the country. The Nandigram police firing in West Bengal, peasant movement in Singur of Hoogly district in West Bengal against the car plant by TATA Motors and police firing in Kalinga Nagar of Jajpur district in Orissa against the Adivasis who protested against the construction of the boundary wall of a proposed Tata Steel Plant are the aftermath of the so-called developmental zones. The life of the victims of displacement reveals the fact that Special Economic Zones are becoming Special Eviction Zones or Special Exploitation Zones. The problems of these victims are overlooked by governments, the agents of such zones. Rf. James David, "Special Economic Zones," *Integral Liberation* Vol. 2/No. 3 (September, 2007): 185-189.

gives the impression that economic policies and developmental projects are not targeted at the poor sections of society. In the midst of this structural evil, faith communities often stand as mute spectators legitimising the sinful structure.

Religious Setting

The Indian society is a religiously pluralistic society. Different religious traditions co-exist and promote the values of love, freedom and dignity of human beings. But the secular society, which is religiously sensitive, has been disturbed by communalism. Communalism poses a tremendous threat to the nation's unity and integrity. Communalism disturbs communal harmony and creates hatred among people of diverse religious traditions. Minority communalism is interpreted as separation and secession, while majority communalism breeds brutal and sustained repression of the minorities. Today, religion is politicised for communal interests.[20] The most vulnerable groups in India are the Tribals and the Dalits. Religiously, they are considered as impure and polluted. It is also an undeniable fact that in communal riots, they are used by Hindutva forces to oppress minority communities. Hindutva forces make division among the Dalits and Tribals based on religious traditions. Among them, Christian Tribals[21] and

---

[20] Desrochers, *Towards A New India*, 113-114.

[21] Hindutva forces insist on the cultural assimilation of the Adivasi community into the Hindu mainstream. They also create enmity between Christian and non-Christian Adivasis to break their unity. Rf. A. S. Hemrom, "The Role of Churches towards building up Adivasi Solidarity: The Call for an Ecumenical Task," *NCC Review* Vol. CXXX/No. 2 (February 2004): 65. They intimidate the Christian priests and nuns who work for Adivasi development and threaten Tribal Christians. Vanavasi Kalyan Ashrams are engaged among the Adivasis to promote hate campaign against Christian minorities. Rf. Ram Puniyani, "Common Minimum Programme and Outcome of Secularism," *Social Action* Vol. 56/No.3 (July-September, 2006): 291.

Dalits[22] suffer a lot due to their conversion. Even though religious freedom is guaranteed by the Indian constitution, the Dalits and the Tribals are deprived of that freedom because of communal forces. Anti-conversion bills are targeted against their conversion.

The call for minority rights is another trend in the religious context of India. Usually, if there is any communal violence, political parties and minority communities uphold minority rights to bring the attention of the government to the protection of minority communities. Today, the emphasis on minority rights has reduced to protect the rights and privileges of minorities, especially the management of educational institutions. If the government interferes in the affairs of minority educational institutions to ensure transparent dealings regarding admission and appointment, minority communities, especially the Christians, raise voice for minority rights. The Christian Church in Kerala fought with the government in its attempts to control self-financing professional colleges. They even issued pastoral letters against the government.[23] The

---

[22] Dalit Christians, because of their religious identity, face discrimination at three levels. Firstly, as 'Dalits' they are discriminated in all aspects even though they are Christians. Secondly, discrimination from governments regarding equal reservation for Dalit Christians. Because of their religion, Dalit Christians cannot enjoy the privileges of Dalits in India. Thirdly, discrimination within the Church from the hands of fellow Christians who continue to claim their high-caste status. Rf. James Massey, "An Analysis of the Dalit Situation....," 70-74.

[23] M. G.Radha Krishnan, "Ire of the Minorities," *India Today* Vol. XXXIII/No. 1 (January 1-7, 2008): 21. The Kerala Professional Colleges (Prevention of Capitation Fee, Regulation of non-exploitative Fee and other measures to ensure Equity and Excellence in professional education) Bill passed by the Kerala Legislative Assembly was opposed by the Mainline Syrian Christian Churches in Kerala. Their protest against the bill was in different forms, such as rallies, public meetings, litigation, closing of schools and issuing of Pastoral Letters. The Pastoral Letters were opposed in and outside the Church because the new Bill

minority communities of West Bengal also conducted mass rally under the banner of United Minority Forum against government interference in the management of minority institutions.[24] In short, religion has been politicised for communal interests and life realities of people have not been the concern of faith communities. By arguing for minority rights to establish the privileges of minority status without any concern for the people who are under various oppressive structures, the Church identity has become a communal entity.

Political Witness of the Church in India: Introspection

The political witness of the Church towards socio-political-economic-religious realities and issues of the Indian society has been communal in nature. It is an undeniable fact that contemporary Christian community, because of its too much minority syndrome, fails to respond to the life of people who are outside the Church. Today's Church is concerned about issues like safeguarding its minority privileges, freedom to profess religion and protection of institutions. Instead of becoming an agent of transformation, the Church seems to be a self-defensive community rather than a community of liberation. Though Church leaders exhort the people to work for the welfare of all citizens and the preservation of civic rights, their focus in actual practice is limited to the people who follow their religious tradition. The Church is politically vigilant whenever the interests of the Christian community

---

was progressive and revolutionary that helps the economically marginalised sections to do professional studies. Rf. George Zachariah, "The Grand Inquisitor and the Syrian Christian Primates in Kerala: Musings on the Pastoral Letter," *Gurukul Journal of Theological Studies* Vol. XVIII/ No.1 (January, 2007): 40-41 & 47.

[24] N. B. Mitra, "Bishops Condemn Govt. Assault on Minority Rights," *People's Reporter* Vol. 20/No. 3 (February 10-25, 2007): 3.

are threatened by the policies and programmes of respective governments and communal-fascist forces. The exclusive privileges enjoyed by the Christian community in the name of minority rights often forget the fact that privileges are to serve fellow beings but not to misuse for economic and political benefits.

The voice of the Church is seldom heard in the struggles of people who are under the plight of oppressive structures like caste and patriarchy. The evil elements of caste and patriarchy dominate even the Church. The Church does not often respond to such issues; it keeps silent and engages with issues in the Christian community. The issues of poverty, child labour, exploitation of women, the displacement of Dalits, Tribals and other communities, etc., are not the real concerns of the Church. They are merely the topics of conferences and seminars conducted by the Church. The political voice of the Church with regard to these issues is not raised in proper forums. Moreover, the Church is hesitant to engage with these issues in its political witness. The tendency of communal politics can also be seen in the life of the Church. Wherever the Christian community is powerful, the political strategies of the Church are supportive of the interests of the community. The Church's political witness has become limited to establish its own rights and privileges and to protect the minority status. The demand for minority rights causes religious communalism. Though the Church politically involves in the efforts to get Dalit Christians legitimate reservation, the entire community is not fully participating. It is also alleged that the institutions of the Church are not accessible to the poor marginalised people because of its 'profit oriented mission.' In short, the problem of the Indian Church in its weak response to human issues is the closed community consciousness that comes out of its theological self-understanding. Therefore, the communal politics of the Church is a theological problem. The pertinent issues faced by people compel the Church to go back to the true nature and to search for a new identity. It challenges the Church to affirm the life of all in society. The political witness of the Church with communal consciousness could be influenced by the classical understanding that limits the life of the Church within the fellowship of believers.

Ecclesiological Debate

The Church in the New Testament is identified as the community of Jesus' followers (1 Cori 1:1-2). It is also referred to as the body of believers (Eph 4: 4). In creedal terms, the Church is defined as the 'one holy, catholic and apostolic church' in the Nicene Constantinopolitan creed of 381.[25] Protestants generally believe that the Church exists "where the word of God is rightly preached and the sacraments are rightly administered."[26] Against the Gnostics, Irenaeus taught that "the Church is the unique sphere of the Holy spirit possessing the canon of truth in apostolic succession focused in the Roman Church."[27] Augustine declares that, on the one hand, the Church is a fellowship of love; on the other hand, it is a mixed community of good and bad. Martin Luther understands the Church in two ways: The Church as a visible fellowship, which includes saints and sinners, and the Church as a hidden community of true believers. For him, the visible church is the embodiment of Gospel. The Eastern Orthodox understanding is that the Church is a community gathered around the Bishop at the Eucharist.[28] In line with the classical

---

[25] John H. Leith, "Ecclesiology," in *A New Hand Book of Christian Theology*, edited by Donald W. Musser and Joseph L. Prince (Nashville: Abingdon Press, 1992), 136.

[26] *Ibid.*, 137.

[27] Richard P. Mcbrien, "Church," *A New Dictionary of Christian Theology*, edited by Alan Richardson and John Bowden (London: SCM Press Ltd, 1983), 109.

[28] *Ibid.*

description, Sadhu Sunder Singh understood the Church as the whole body of those who belong to Christ.[29] A. J. Appasamy also defined the Church as the Body of Christ. It is an instrument of God's rule and another medium of revealing His will in the world.[30] The classical understanding of the Church is pictured as a community of holy ones that hold the truth of divine revealed in Jesus and become alive through the Word of God and the sacraments. Here the implied notion is that the focus of the Church is not the people as such but rituals and practices.

Vatican II was a turning point in the perception of the Church. It officially described the Church "as a mystery or sacrament, as the whole people of God, as a collegial reality .... as having a mission not only to proclaim the kingdom of God in Word and sacrament, but to be itself a credible sign and example of that kingdom as well as an instrument of its realization in the world at large through its service on behalf of justice and peace."[31] Before Vatican II, the Church was depicted as the only hope of salvation. From Vatican II onwards, the Church was sought to be seen as a sign and sacrament of salvation. Liberation theologians tried to find the identity of the Church in siding with the poor to witness the liberating action of God.[32] Leonardo Boff calls the Church as a community and sign of liberation.[33] The liberation

---

[29] Robin Boyd, *An Introduction to Indian Christian Theology* (Delhi: ISPCK, 2005), 105.

[30] *Ibid.*, 142.

[31] Richard P. Mcbrien, "Church," 110.

[32] Letty M. Russel, *Church in the Round* (Louisville: Westminister/ John Knox Press, 1993), 43.

[33] Leonardo Boff, *Church: Charism and Power* (New York: The Cross Road Publishing Company, 1988), 134-135.

ecclesiology paved the way for new developments in ecclesiology, such as Feminist Ecclesiology and Dalit Ecclesiology. Feminist Ecclesiology reflects the Church as "a community of Christ, bought with price, where everyone is welcome."[34] It explores and emphasises the relation between the experience of people who are struggling for the full humanity of all women together with men, and the experience of those who struggle for liberation and new life in biblical and Church tradition.[35] Dalit ecclesiology holds that "Dalit Church is a messianic community which witness to the incarnate Lord who identified himself totally with the Dalitness of his people. The identity of a Dalit Church is not only determined by all those who are oppressed, but also those who participate in the liberation of the oppressed.[36] The liberation ecclesiologies highlighted the Church as a worldly reality that responds to the life experiences of people and as a community that identifies and works for the liberation of oppressed communities. A similar position can be seen in M.M. Thomas: "Church is the foretaste and prophetic sign of the New Humanity created in Christ. The Church must be present wherever renewal of humanity takes place."[37] In tune with these visions, Paulose Mar Paulose interpreted the Church as a powerful and important tool in God's revolutionary strategy.[38] He placed political witness as a means

---

[34] Letty M. Russel, *Church in the Round*, 43.

[35] *Ibid.*, 18.

[36] Manchala DeenaBandhu, *"Towards a Dalit Ecclesiology An Examination of the Writings of Select Dalit Theologians"* (M.Th. Thesis, Senate of Serampore College, 1994), 81.

[37] M.M. Thomas, *The Gospel of Forgiveness and Koinonia* (Delhi: ISPCK and Thiruvalla: CSS, 1994), 44.

[38] Paulose Mar Paulose, *Church's Mission* (Bombay: BUILD, n.d.), 2.

of responding to the aspirations of the marginalised to realise God's revolutionary strategy. Indeed, the nature and vocation of the Church is to respond to people in their existential realities.

Chapter 2
The Ecclesiology of Dietrich Bonhoeffer

Dietrich Bonhoeffer, a German theologian, is known for his theological praxis during the Nazi regime. He developed his own theological convictions as a faith response to his context and challenged the Christian community to the praxis of costly discipleship. Bonhoeffer was particularly interested in the life and public witness of the Church. His ecclesiology not only transcended the religious realm, but also engaged with social realities and the questions of the time. He emphasised the creative relationship of the Church with the State as an important aspect of the Church's witness in society. Bonhoeffer's ecclesiology has influenced many theologians and church leaders throughout the world.

Dietrich Bonhoeffer: The Man and His Context

Dietrich Bonhoeffer was born on February 4, 1906, in Broslau, Germany, which is now part of Poland, as the son of Karl Ludwing and Paula Bonhoeffer. His father was a scientifically trained medical practitioner. Karl Friedrich, his elder brother, was a physical chemist and Klaus, another brother, was a lawyer.[1] His family was not happy with his decision to enter into the ministry of the Church. He began his studies at Tubingen, and after one year, in 1924, he joined the University of Berlin. In 1927, Bonhoeffer submitted his dissertation, "A Dogmatic Investigation of the Sociology of the Church." After his studies, he worked as a pastor for two years in Barcelona. In 1931, he was elected as the International Youth Secretary for the World Alliance of Churches. This new responsibility gave Bonhoeffer enough opportunities to travel different parts of the world and to share about Hitler's persecution of the Church.[2] The year 1932 was a turning point in the life of Bonhoeffer when Adolf Hitler came into power in Germany. Bonhoeffer strongly responded against the Aryan Clause passed by the German Reichstag in April, 1933, which called for the exclusion of Jews from Government service. Surprisingly, the German Reich Church also accepted the Aryan Clause in its ministry appointments. His response to the Aryan Clause was expressed in 'The Church and the Jewish Question', where he asserted that in the current political climate, the Church is forced not simply to "bandage the victims under the wheel, but to jam the spoke in the wheel itself."[3] The Church has 'an unconditional obligation' to the victims of society irrespective of their religious affiliations. Bonhoeffer also criticised the Nazi theologians' "disinheritance theory", which explains that the Jews lost their divine election

---

[1] Carl Friedrich von Weizsacker, "Thoughts of a Non-Theologian on Dietrich Bonhoeffer's Theological Development," *The Ecumenical Review* Vol. 28/No. 2 (April 1976): 157.

[2] Dallas M. Roark, *Dietrich Bonhoeffer* (London: Word Books, 1975), 14-17.

[3] Charles Marsh, "Dietrich Bonhoeffer," in *The Modern Theologians*, edited by David F. Ford (Oxford: Blackwell Publishers, 1997), 38.

by rejecting the identity of Jesus as the messiah. In *The Bethel Confession* of August 1933, he defended the Jews and opposed the attempt of the German Evangelical Church to become a national Church of Christians by Aryan descent. In 1935, he helped the Confessing Church, the Church formed at Barmen in 1934 in opposition to the German Reich Church's adoption of the Aryan Clause, to start a seminary, which was later closed down by the German secret police.[4] Because of his opposition to Nazi administration, restrictions were imposed on Bonhoeffer to preach or lecture in Berlin. When things became so difficult, Bonhoeffer left for United States of America in 1939 to teach at the Union Theological Seminary, New York. But the tyranny of the Nazi rule in Germany compelled him to return to his homeland. Explaining his decision to leave the Union Theological Seminary, Bonhoeffer wrote to Reinhold Niebuhr: "I shall have no right to participate in the reconstruction of Christian life in Germany after the war, if I do not share the trials of this time with my people."[5]

Dietrich Bonhoeffer returned to Nazi Germany when it was completely under war with the Allied Forces. The Nazi regime demanded total commitment from the people. The German Reich Church supported the policies of Hitler. Bonhoeffer was forbidden to preach or teach. The Jews were under terror and threat. They were either treated cruelly or killed or forced to leave Germany. But Bonhoeffer supported the Jews in all possible ways. The seminary students were also forced to join the army service. Germany was literally under the situation of arson, forced death, murder, lies, suffering,

---

[4] *Ibid.*

[5] Stanly J. Grenz and Roger E. Olson, *20th Century Theology* (Secunderabad: OM Books, 1992), 148.

and extermination camps.⁶ Bonhoeffer describes the Nazi rule: "It was the concrete suffering of injustice, of the organized lie, of hostility to mankind, and of violence; it was the persecution of lawfulness, truth, humanity, and freedom...."⁷ He also faced with military service and worked as a courier in the Intelligence Service of Gestapo. While he was working in military service, he supported certain members of the German Military Intelligence Service who opposed Hitler, and conspired to assassinate him. Being a pacifist, the main reason for supporting the plot was his severe disappointment with the efforts of the Confessing Church and the Ecumenical Church towards internal and external peace.⁸ But on April 5, 1943, Bonhoeffer was arrested along with his colleagues in the Intelligence Service for helping the Jews to escape Germany and was taken to Tegel military prison in Berlin. In July 1944, again, Bonhoeffer was arrested in the background of another attempt on Hitler's life and was transferred to the Prinz-Albrecht Street Gestapo prison. On April 8, 1945, at Flossenburg, at an extermination camp, he was trialed and sentenced to death. On April 9, 1945, he was executed, a week before Hitler's suicide.⁹ His theological contributions remain as a source of inspiration even after his birth centenary.¹⁰ Bonhoeffer's involvement in the ecumenical movement and

---

⁶ Movie-*Bonhoeffer, Agent of Grace*. Winner of Best Film at Monte Carlo Television Festival 2000.

⁷ Quoted in Larry.L.Rasmussen, *Dietrich Bonhoeffer, Reality and Resistance* (Louisville: Westminster John Knox Press, 2005), 33.

⁸ *Ibid.*, 62.

⁹ Dallas M. Roark, *Dietrich Bonhoeffer*, 22-23.

¹⁰ His important works are *Act and Being* (London: Harper and Row Publishers, 1961); *Creation and Fall* (London: Mac Millan Publishing Company, 1964); *The Cost of Discipleship* (London: SCM Press, 1949) *Ethics* (New York: Mac Millan Company, 1962) *Letters and Papers from Prison* (New York: Mac Millan Publishing Company, 1972) etc.

the resistance movement brought him respect from the global Christian community. Through his words and actions, he encouraged the Church to witness Christ in all spheres of life.

Major Influences on the Theological Development of Dietrich Bonhoeffer

In his theological development, Dietrich Bonhoeffer was influenced by many factors. His family, his life at the Union Theological Seminary, his friendship with Reinhold Niebuhr, the Black Church, theologians, writers, etc., influenced his theological journey immensely. John D. Godsey identifies three qualities in Bonhoeffer that played major roles at every point in his life: A remarkable vitality, an unusually sensitive nature and a capacity for turning thought into action.[11] At Tubingen, Adolf Schlatter, who taught him the Jewish background of the New Testament, influenced him, and it helped him later on to defend against the anti-Jewish campaign in the German academy.[12] Ernest Troeltsch, the theologian and philosopher and a frequent guest at Bonhoeffer's home, also made a great impact on him. His pastoral ministry in Barcelona after his studies gave him the opportunity to associate with people.[13] Apart from these factors, the following are some of the major influences on him.

Family

Bonhoeffer's family contributed much to his intellectual development. His father was a medical doctor and a leading authority on psychiatry and neurology. His brothers were

---

[11] John D. Godsey, *The Theology of Dietrich Bonhoeffer* (London: SCM Press Ltd, 1960), 20.

[12] Mary Bosanquent, *The Life and Death of Dietrich Bonhoeffer* (London: Hodder and Stoughton, 1968), 50.

[13] Dallas M. Roark, *Dietrich Bonhoeffer*, 16.

highly qualified professionals in law and physical chemistry. Bonhoeffer's parents were clear-sighted, educated people and were inflexible in all things that matter in life. He inherited honesty, fairness, self-control and aptitude from his father. His unshakeable commitment, sympathy, great human understanding and devotion to the cause of the oppressed were the influence of his mother.[14] Though his mother instructed him elementary religious customs, she did not insist on him involving in the Church. Though his brothers' criticism about the Church as a poor, feeble, boring, petty bourgeois institution created a sense of suspicion about the Church in Bonhoeffer, it also inspired him to say: "In that case, I shall reform it."[15] The family gave him an atmosphere where he was able to absorb the different trends of the time.

Bonhoeffer's Life in the United States of America

Bonhoeffer's life at the Union Theological Seminary, New York, influenced him to do theology with a concern for the poor and the needy. His life in the USA also helped him to think about ecumenism and the relation between the State and the Church. His contact with Jean Lassere, a French Reformed pastor and a friend at Union Theological Seminary, influenced him to change his nationalistic attitude towards war and his negative attitude towards the ecumenical movement.[16] In the US, Bonhoeffer saw strict separation between the State and the Church, yet the Church was passionately concerned with the social, economic and political affairs of the State.[17] His

---

[14] G. Leibholz "Memoir" in Dietrich Bonhoeffer, *The Cost of Discipleship* (Bombay: St. Paul Publications, 1974, Indian Edition), 9.

[15] Charles Marsh, "Dietrich Bonhoeffer," 37.

[16] Dallas M. Roark, *Dietrich Bonhoeffer*, 16.

[17] John D. Godsey, *The Theology of Dietrich Bonhoeffer*, 25-26.

exposure to the Black Church[18] must have influenced him to do theology in the context of his people, who suffered political discrimination and violation of human rights under the Nazi rule as the Blacks experienced socio-racial discrimination under the White supremists. His experiences with the Black churches of Harlem taught him the importance of the Church in the lives of people, particularly the value of fellowship, and motivated him to return to the Church.[19] Bonhoeffer was further exposed to neo-orthodoxy through Reinhold Niebuhr, his colleague at the Union Theological Seminary. Niebuhr emphasised on the cross of Christ, and coupled it with an active political theology. Bonhoeffer believed that both are equally needed.[20] The experiences in the US had a strong influence on Bonhoeffer to work for the unity of the Church to stand against the dehumanising power structures that devalue human freedom. He also learned about the vocation of the Church towards the poor and the State. He was also exposed to the neo-orthodoxy that challenged him to have a Christo-centric response to social systems.

Adolf von Harnack

For Bonhoeffer, Adolf von Harnack, the eminent historian and theologian of the Church, was both neighbour and teacher. He was one of his father's colleagues. Harnack considered the meaning of Christianity as not depending on theological dogmatism but in the understanding of religion as a historical development. The Christian doctrine is an outcome of the

---

[18] Dietrich Bonhoeffer, *No Rusty Swords* (New York: Harper & Row Publishers, 1965), 112-113.

[19] Jay C. Rochelle, "Bonhoeffer: Community, Authority and Spirituality," *Currents in Theology and Mission* Vol. 21/No.2 (April, 1994), 121.

[20] Dietrich Bonhoeffer, *No Rusty Swords*, 116.

Hellenistic-Greek spirit based on the Gospel of Jesus. The recovery of the essence of the Gospel from the dogma can be completed through the historical-critical approach. If Christianity wants to be relevant in the modern context, it must be freed from any connection with the dogmas that are identified with the Hellenistic world.[21] Though Bonhoeffer rejected Harnack's theological method, he was much impressed by his enthusiasm for truth and intellectual integrity. Harnack helped him to understand the German liberal tradition. The questions that Bonhoeffer articulated in his concept of 'Religionless Christianity' were the result of the influence of liberal theology taught by Harnack.[22]

Karl Barth

Like Karl Barth, Bonhoeffer also kept a decisive break with the liberalism of his theology teachers. He believed that God's revelation is only in and through Jesus Christ, and the heart of theology and ethics is divine self-disclosure. But at the same time, Bonhoeffer rejected the radical views of Karl Barth. Bonhoeffer saw a closer link between Christ and the Church than Barth did in his theology. It is observed that the Barthian influence of the 'theology of the Word of God' can be seen in the theology of Bonhoeffer.[23] As Kennet Hamilton opines, "If there is one key that opens the door to his theology more than any other, it is the recognition that at all stages of his career he consciously formed his own concepts with Barth in mind

---

[21] Encyclopedia Britannica, "Adolf von Harnack," *http://www.britannica.com/eb/article-9001567/Adolf-von-Harnack*, 7-09-2007, 3.57 PM.

[22] Matt Mc Laughlin, "Dietrich Bonhoeffer," httt://people.bu.edu. /wwildman/Weird Wild Web/courses/mwt/dictionary/mut-themes-780-bonhoeffer.htm, 7-09-2007, 3.30 PM.

[23] Stanly J. Grenz and Roger E. Olson, *20th Century Theology,* 150.

more than any other living theologians."[24] The theological relationship of Bonhoeffer with Karl Barth was one of motivation and ideological corrective.[25] In short, Karl Barth influenced Bonhoeffer to develop a Christo-centric theology that corresponded to the reality of the world.

Friedrich Naumann

Friedrich Naumann, a political and social theorist and reformer, who was one of the partisans of German Liberalism, influenced Bonhoeffer to think about the union between faith and life. As a teenager, Bonhoeffer read a book of Friedrich Naumann entitled *Letters on Religion*. For Naumann, genuine Christianity was an ideal that never touched down into the real lived experience of the people. Bonhoeffer was haunted by this thesis and it became useful knowledge for developing his Christian faith. Bonhoeffer's struggle with this problem led him to propose the union between faith and life in his famous work, *The Cost of Discipleship*.[26]

---

[24] *Ibid.*

[25] This relationship can be summed up in three segments. Firstly, Barth's dialectical theology. Bonhoeffer saw Barthian dialectical theology as problematic because it explains an infinite qualitative distinction between human experience and God's incomprehensible mystery. It challenged Bonhoeffer to argue that God's act of becoming human shows the intention of God to relate with the realities of people and to be intelligible to all creation. Secondly, Barth's thinking of the relation between God and human beings helped Bonhoeffer to resolve the conflict between act and being. Barth's saying 'God's being is in his act' taught Bonhoeffer that the ontology of the relation between God and human beings is the revelation of God in Jesus Christ. Thirdly, his interaction with Barth's theology that gives less importance to the worldliness of the world led Bonhoeffer to affirm that the reality of God and the reality of world cannot be separated because in Christ both are reconciled. Rf. Charles Marsh, "Dietrich Bonhoeffer," 39.

[26] Jay C. Rochelle, "Bonhoeffer: Community, Authority and Spirituality," 117.

Luther's Doctrine of the Two Kingdoms

Luther's doctrine of the Two Kingdoms can be traced back to the Augustinian conception of the 'Two Cities.'[27] Luther's idea of two kingdoms[28] was against the Catholic understanding of the two kingdoms—the Spiritual and the Secular. He did not see the secular and the sacred as separate and unrelated areas. Luther says that "for all Christians really and truly belong to the religious class, and there is no difference among them except in so far as they have different offices.... because we have one baptism, Gospel and faith. Those who exercise secular authority have been baptized like rest of us."[29] Here the distinction is based on different tasks than personal qualifications. But in the context of Christians and people of other faiths, Luther made a distinction between people who belonged to the Kingdom of God (Christians) and people who belonged to the Kingdom of the World (people of other faiths). These are the Two Kingdoms. Since all people do not believe in God and oppose evil, God has set up two forms of rule—the spiritual and the secular. In the secular authority, it is not necessary that the emperor should be a Christian. The role of the secular authority is to manage worldly affairs but not otherworldly matters. Christians should be subject to the secular authority as long as they are responsible rulers.[30] As a Lutheran, Bonhoeffer was also influenced by Luther's doctrine of the Two Kingdoms. It can be noticed in his pacifist approach, his understanding of the State as divinely constituted and his resistance against the Nazi rule.

---

[27] Saint Augustine, *The City of God* (New York: Image Books, Double Day, 1958).

[28] *Works of Martin Luther* Vol. IV (Philadelphia: Muhlenberg Press, 1931), 265f.

[29] Gerhard Ebeling, *Luther, An Introduction to His Thought* (Philadelphia: Fortress Press, 1980), 180.

[30] *Ibid.*, 183-187.

Theological Method of Dietrich Bonhoeffer

Bonhoeffer developed his theology in a particular context with the support of diverse sources such as Scripture, tradition and experience. He extensively used biblical resources in his theological constructions. For example, *The Cost of Discipleship* is a commentary on Matthew 12:30 and *Ethics* and *Letters and Papers from Prison* are commentaries on Mark 9:40.[31] Bonhoeffer's pacifist position till 1939 was the result of his adherence to the German Lutheran tradition.[32] But his passive resistance became active resistance in the context of the failure of the German Church. It is evident in his work, *Letters and Papers from Prison*, which represents a radical discontinuity with the tradition.[33] The experiences of Bonhoeffer in the US and in Nazi Germany in particular are an important source of the theological shifts in him.[34]

In spite of the fact that Bonhoeffer was not a systematic theologian, a theological method could be perceived from his theological articulations. In his early lectures on 'Christology' presented in *Christ the Center*, Bonhoeffer depicted Jesus as the mediator of all reality. When the German Church had begun to identify Christ with the Aryan ideals, Bonhoeffer sought to shift the basic Christological question from "How can Jesus Christ be both God and human?" to "Who is he?" During this time, he realised that Christology proceeds not from abstract notions like logos or being, but from the historical Jesus of Nazareth, crucified and resurrected from

---

[31] Larry. L. Rasmussen, *Dietrich Bonhoeffer, Reality and Resistance*, 36.

[32] *Ibid.*, 58 &130.

[33] Douglas John Hall, *Remembered Voices* (Louisville: West minster John Knox Press, 1998), 67.

[34] Movie - *Bonhoeffer, Agent of Grace*.

the dead.[35] It is also difficult to separate Christology from Ecclesiology in the theology of Bonhoeffer. In Bonhoeffer, we could see the parallel of "Jesus the man for others" and the "Church existing for others." Jesus the man for others is present in the Church that exists for others. Here the methodological formula of Bonhoeffer's theologising starts with the question 'How is Christ taking form in the world?' or 'Who is Christ for us today?' and ends with an answer to the question, 'What am I to do?'[36] It shows that Bonhoeffer was contextual and Christo-centric in his theological reflections. A theological method can also be traced from his activities and writings, i.e., Contextual Christo-centrism. It means that Bonhoeffer built up his theological propositions by answering 'Who is Jesus Christ for us today?' in the light of contextual challenges. Bonhoeffer did his ecclesiology in line with this method.

The Ecclesiology of Bonhoeffer

Bonhoeffer developed his ecclesiology based on the concept of the Body of Christ (1 Cor. 12: 13ff and Gal. 3: 28). He built up his ecclesiology in the context of Church-State tensions in Nazi Germany. He also drew from Luther's idea of 'Church as a community' to expand his concept of Church. For Luther, Church is not only a place for the interpretation of text, but also a place for the oral proclamation of the Word. Such a theological position is evident in Bonhoeffer's understanding of the Church as community.[37]

---

[35] Charles Marsh, "Dietrich Bonhoeffer," 45.

[36] Larry. L. Rasmussen, *Dietrich Bonhoeffer, Reality and Resistance*, 22-23.

[37] Jay C. Rochelle, "Bonhoeffer: Community, Authority and Spirituality," 121-122.

Church: A Reality in the World

According to Bonhoeffer, "Christ is present in the Church. This Church is no ideal Church but a reality in the world, a bit of the world reality. The secularity of the Church follows from the incarnation of Christ. The Church like Christ, has become the world."[38] It means the Church has all the weaknesses and sufferings of the world. The Church, like Christ himself, must be without any security. For the sake of people, the Church must be a worldly reality. It is a worldly reality for all people. The worldly reality, the real secularity consists in the Church's being able to renounce all privileges and all its possessions for the sake of people but not Christ's Word and the forgiveness of sins.[39]

> The Church...remains the Church of the baptized, and therefore a communion of sinners. All baptized persons belong to it, no matter what their works may seem to be. Renunciation of its claims to "purity" leads the Church back to its solidarity with this sinful world. It has as its place not only with the poor but also with the rich; not only with the pious, but also with the Godless.[40]

The faith of the Church is for both the outcast and the rich. So the Church that stands for all people in the world and that confesses its secularity can claim to be an *ecclesia perfecta* or perfect Church.[41] Bonhoeffer also affirms that "the Church

---

[38] Quoted from Dietrich Bonhoeffer, *A Testament to Freedom: The Essential Writings of Dietrich Bonhoeffer*, edited by Geffrey B. Kelly and F. Burton Nelson (San Francisco: Harper-Sanfrancisco, 1995), 86-87 in Carla Barnhill, *A Year with Dietrich Bonhoeffer* (New York: HarperCollins, 2005), 178.

[39] *Ibid.*

[40] *Ibid.*, 180.

[41] *Ibid.*

can only defend its own space by fighting, not for space, but for the salvation of the world. Otherwise the Church becomes a 'religious society' that fights in its own interest and thus has ceased to be the Church of God in the world."[42] So the primary task of the Church is not to stand for its own cause but to become the witness of Jesus Christ in the world.[43] For Bonhoeffer, witness of the Church means, "The Church is the Church only when it exists for others."[44] Bonhoeffer depicts the Church as a reality that fully involves in the world by raising voices for the entire humanity and by embodying Jesus in the hopes and aspirations of the people.

Church: Christ Existing as Community

Bonhoeffer observes that "the Church is 'Christ existing as community,' and is to be understood as a collective person."[45] For him, the Church is the community of the Lord Jesus Christ, and its territory is the whole world. The Church is the universal community in the world. It is the presence of Christ on earth and is called as *Christus praesens*. The word of the present Christ is the word of the Church to the people in the world. The word of the Church must encounter all the realities of the world.[46] In Bonhoeffer's theology, the Church is more than a religious fellowship; it has social and political dimensions. He envisioned a Church that upheld the values of social and political life and motivated the State to put them into practice. In his understanding, the Church was Christ himself and was

---

[42] Quoted from Dietrich Bonhoeffer, *Ethics* (Minneapolis: Fortress Press, 2005), 63-64 in Carla Barnhill, *A Year with Dietrich Bonhoeffer*, 21.

[43] *Ibid.*

[44] Dietrich Bonhoeffer, *Letters and Papers from Prison* (New York: Macmillan Publishing, 1972), 382.

[45] Dietrich Bonhoeffer, *No Rusty Swords*, 33.

[46] *Ibid.*, 161.

called to new life. Because of the socio-political responsibility, says Bonhoeffer, "Church is not a religious community of worshippers of Christ but is Christ Himself who has taken form among men. The Church is the man in Christ and awakened to new life."[47]

The Church as 'Christ existing as community,' for Bonhoeffer, is for maintaining Christian piety and morality. It must be preserved to serve the people, the order and the State. It upholds sacrifice, prayer and forgiveness. It proclaims life in death, shares love in hate, brings the message of salvation in suffering and hope in despair.[48] So the Church is the preached and the preaching Christ, proclamation and proclaimer, office from God and Word. It is the communion of saints who are freed by God to become responsible persons who hear and give themselves for others in the world.[49] Bonhoeffer also attempted to relate this 'Christ existing community' with societal life in his theology. That is why he emphasised that the Church can be a true Church only when it exists for humanity.[50] By highlighting the Church as 'Christ existing as community,' Bonhoeffer interpreted the mission of Jesus as the ministry of the Church in the world. That means Bonhoeffer's ecclesiology goes beyond the traditional understanding of the Church to the realities of human community. As a presence of Christ on earth, the Church is responsible for the flourishing of humanity.

---

[47] Dietrich Bonhoeffer, *Ethics* (New York: Macmillan Company, 1962), 21.

[48] Dietrich Bonhoeffer, *No Rusty Swords*, 154-155.

[49] *Ibid.*, 154.

[50] John D. Godsey, *The Theology of Dietrich Bonhoeffer*, 259.

Church: A Visible Body of Jesus Christ

In his ecclesiology, Bonhoeffer interpreted the Church as the visible body of Jesus Christ. For him, the body of the Lord is also visible in the form of the Church. Jesus became visible through the preaching of the Word and the sacraments of Baptism and Lord's Supper. Since the Church experiences these visible signs, it becomes the visible body of Jesus Christ in the world.[51] Bonhoeffer's emphasis on the Church, the visible body of Christ, reminds that "the Church is not a religious community of those who revere Christ but Christ who has taken form among human beings."[52] The Church cannot claim anything other than that of the form of Jesus Christ. The Church is nothing but the place in the world or the part of humanity where Christ really has taken the form. Therefore, the basic concern of the Church is not to protect the so-called religious functions of human beings, but to engage with the existential crisis of human beings. It demands the participation of the Church in the human realities to reveal the true nature and identity of Christ.[53] Through preaching the Word and administering the sacraments, Jesus Christ is taking form among the people because the Word and the sacraments are from Christ. The visible signs show his concern for the entire humanity. In sum, being a visible body of Christ means being involved in the world through the life of Jesus.

Church and State

The Church and its relation to the State are important aspects in the ecclesiology of Bonhoeffer. He developed an ecclesiology

---

[51] Dietrich Bonhoeffer, *The Cost of Discipleship* (London: SCM Press Ltd, 1959), 223-26.

[52] Quoted from Dietrich Bonhoeffer, *Ethics* (Minneapolis: Fortress Press, 2005), 96-97 in Carla Barnhill, *A Year with Dietrich Bonhoeffer*, 354.

[53] *Ibid.*

that supports the Church-State relationship, which is relevant even in the present context. Bonhoeffer's understanding of the Church-State relationship is based on Scripture (1 Cor. 8: 6, Col. 1: 16, 17, 20, Jn. 1: 3) and Luther's idea of two kingdoms. For him, both the Church and the State are manifestations of divine presence. "Christ is present to us in a double form as church and as state. And Christ as the centre of history is the mediator between the State and God, in the form of the Church."[54] Bonhoeffer states that the Church is also the centre of the State. "Since Christ is present in the Church after the cross and the resurrection, this Church too must be understood as the centre of history. It is the centre of a history which is made by the State. The Church is the hidden centre of the sphere of the State."[55] Since Christ represents the Church and the State, both are bound by the same Lord and are united together. Though the State and the Church have distinct functions, both have the same area of function: human beings.[56] As Christ is the foundation of the Church and the State, both are called to struggle against the destructive forces in society. To fight against the vicious elements in the human community, the Church and the State have a political responsibility to help each other.

The Church and the State: Mutual Accountability

In Bonhoeffer's ecclesiology, the Church and the State represent the presence of Christ. Though both are working for the betterment of humanity, they correct each other and are expected to work in accordance with their own special tasks. The State demands obedience from the Church. It also

---

[54] Dietrich Bonhoeffer, *Christology* (London: Collins, 1966), 66.

[55] *Ibid.*, 65.

[56] Dietrich Bonhoeffer, *Ethics*, 315.

demands the Church not to interfere in the affairs of the secular office. For Bonhoeffer, the State can demand the spiritual office to desist its interference in the secular office. At the same time, since the spiritual office is very much related to public, the State can supervise it as part of observing the outward justice. The State can thus interfere in the spiritual office in connection with matters of justice.[57] Here the State is depicted as a secular authority that is not controlled by any religion. It functions in the light of divine justice.

The Church has the task of testifying before the State to their common master—Jesus Christ. Also, the Church is responsible for summoning the whole world to submit to the dominion of Jesus Christ. It does not mean that the aim of the Church is to pursue the State to follow a Christian policy or enact Christian laws. The Church expects the State to be faithful to its responsibilities. In relation to the claims on the State, the Church demands protection for public Christian proclamation against violence and blasphemy, protection for the institution of the Church against arbitrary interference and protection for Christian life in obedience to Jesus Christ.[58] It should be understood in the light of human rights and religious freedom. From these claims, it can be assumed that the Church's witness in society is to become a corrective force by sacrificing its own interests and by upholding Christian values that stand for all people.

The Ecclesiastical Responsibility of the State

In Bonhoeffer's theology of State, the State should be independent of religious decisions. It should protect righteous actions and should be neutral in religious matters. The State should not become the foundation of a new religion because

---

[57] *Ibid.*, 310-311.

[58] *Ibid.*

it will affect the functions of the State. The State is also responsible for giving protection to religious communities. In order to avoid conflict due to the differences between various forms of service of God, the State should take care of those situations. Bonhoeffer's emphasis on religious conflicts shows that he is against religious confrontations. He also does not support the fundamentalist approach of Christian proclamation. For him, if the people who control the government are Christians, they should realise that the Christian proclamation is to be done not by the means of the sword, but by the means of the Word.[59] In the ecclesiastical responsibility of the State, two things are highlighted—the protection of religious communities that is the protection of human communities and the combat against religious fundamentalism. The protection of human communities means safeguarding human rights and privileges. If the State is faithful to its vocation, it can resist religious conflicts. The task of the Church is to demonstrate the divine character of the State and to proclaim the message of the Word, the human liberation, to the world.

The Political Responsibility of the Church

The Church's political responsibility has different dimensions. Since the Church and the State are the two-fold forms of the presence of Christ on earth, the Church has the political task to address and challenge the State. The Church has positive and negative tasks in relation to State affairs. For Bonhoeffer, the Church should call sin by its name and should warn people against sin. The warning against sin should be done to the congregation openly and publicly. It is also the responsibility of the Church to draw the attention of the government to the errors and shortcomings that disrupt the function of the State.

---

[59] *Ibid.*, 312-313.

If the State does not listen to the voice of the Church, the only political responsibility that remains for the Church is to maintain and encourage the order of outward justice at least among its own members. By doing so, the Church is being faithful to its special tasks.[60]

Bonhoeffer encourages the political participation of Christians in nation building. The Church should work for the building up of the State that upholds political values. According to Bonhoeffer, "the Church which may not enter the political struggle must nevertheless enjoin its members to study social questions with the ultimate aim of act."[61] Bonhoeffer also understands that the Church has a prophetic role in its relationship with the State. This aspect can be seen in his essay, 'The Church Before the Jewish Question' where he says, "so long as the State acts to maintain justice and order, the Church as such may not engage in direct political action against the state. This does not mean that the Church takes no interest in political affairs, for it is the responsibility of the Church to ask the State again and again whether it is fulfilling its duties as a state."[62] The Church must also protest against the State in both situations, i.e., when there is 'too little order' and when there is 'too much order.' 'Too little order' means allowing a group to go and live beyond laws. 'Too much order' means suppressing the proclamation of Christian faith.[63] In short, the Church has the responsibility for supporting the State in genuine situations, at the same time to resist the State when it takes improper actions that disrupt community. The Church as 'Christ existing community' is called to become a

---

[60] *Ibid.*, 314.

[61] Dietrich Bonhoeffer, *No Rusty Swords*, 294.

[62] John D. Godsey, *The Theology of Dietrich Bonhoeffer*, 110.

[63] *Ibid.*

corrective and prophetic force that participates in the development of the State through political participation.

Dietrich Bonhoeffer has contributed much to twentieth century theology. His theological reflections continue to influence the Christian communities all over the world. He was formed in a context that was enriched by diverse theological trends, such as German Lutheran tradition, Liberalism and neo-orthodoxy. Although Bonhoeffer was influenced by the socio-political-ecclesiastical framework of his time, he took a different position to articulate his faith. His method of theologising was contextual and Christocentric. With this method, he approached the doctrines of the Church. The theological engagement of Bonhoeffer with human issues was praxis-oriented. In his theology, Bonhoeffer attempted to reflect on the witness of the Church in the context of the Church-State conflict. The ecclesiology of Bonhoeffer was developed in a background in which the Church was striving to protect itself without any concern for others; and the State was trying to bring the Church under its control. His ecclesiology strongly affirms that the Church is Christ's presence, which is called to exist for all people. It is not a communal society but a community of Jesus that encounters world realities. So the Church cannot be silent and kept away from the political activity of the State. The political engagement of the Church in society is not restricted to safeguarding rights. It has accountability to argue for others and to work for the building of a responsible State. Bonhoeffer brought out an ecclesiology that is committed to all aspects of human life.

Chapter 3

Church as New Humanity in Christ: The Ecclesiology of M. M. Thomas

Theological Background of M. M. Thomas

M. M. Thomas, a theologian of the 20th century, shaped his theology for effecting radical changes in the pluralistic context of India. His theological attempt focuses on all dimensions of human life. As an ecumenical theologian, M. M. Thomas formulated his thinking within the inter-religious framework. In his theological pursuit, Thomas interprets Gospel to uphold social justice and human dignity in the context of human rights violation, political oppression, economic exploitation and degradation of social values.

A brief biographical sketch, major influences on the development of his theology and the concept of New Humanity in Christ are discussed in this chapter.

M. M. Thomas: An Ecumenical Lay Theologian

Madathiparampil Mammen Thomas was born into a middle-class family on 15th May 1916 at Kavungumprayar. He was brought up at Kozhencherry in Pathanamthitta District, Kerala. His father was the secretary of a local Co-operative Society and his mother was a school teacher. A member of the Mar Thoma Church, he was brought up in a devout atmosphere in which regular attendance in Church service, prayer meetings, Sunday school and evangelistic piousness at home determined his early journey of faith. When he was fifteen years old, Thomas joined Science College, Trivandrum, as a Chemistry student and graduated in 1935. He actively participated in Mar Thoma Youth Union and Student Christian Movement during his college years at Trivandrum.[1] Thomas explains his personal commitment to Jesus in his *Ente Christava Dharmanveshana Paryadanam* that "it was in the year 1931-32, through an evangelical spiritual experience ... that Jesus Christ became real to me as the bearer of Divine Forgiveness; and gave my life, awakened to adolescent age, a principle of integration and a sense of direction."[2] While he was a student in Trivandrum, he used to visit the neighbouring centres of the city for evangelistic work. After his studies in Trivandrum, he joined Asram High School, Perumpavoor, as teacher. In order to involve more directly in evangelism and social service, Thomas resigned from this school in 1937. He tried to integrate evangelisation and social work in his career. In 1938, Thomas organised a House for Waifs and Strays (Bala Bhavan) on an inter-religious basis. At the same time, he organised a Beggar Relief Committee in co-operation with Trivandrum City Corporation. In 1941, he stopped his work at Bala Bhavan as

---

[1] Hielke T. Wolters, *Theology of Prophetic Participation* (Delhi: ISPCK & Banglore: UTC, 1996), 12.

[2] *Ibid.*, 13.

his fellow workers and members of the Governing Council had blamed him for misusing the House for evangelisation. 'Bala Bhavan' and Young Christian Council of Action (YCCA) helped Thomas to understand social reality and the Christian social tradition. Thomas' involvement in the activities of Bala Bhavan and YCCA was a turning point in his life. He began to consider Gospel in line with the social context.

M.M. Thomas desired to get ordination from Mar Thomas church and membership from Communist Party of India. But this attempt failed in 1943 as the church ordination committee viewed that he was not Christ-centered enough and the party came to the conclusion that his religious conviction would bring disruption to party ranks and pave the way for reactions. What is understood from this experience is that through the ordination from Mar Thoma Church and party membership, M.M. Thomas may have intended to relate his religious convictions with social realities. In the same year, he organised the National Christian Youth Council (NCYC) by combining Christian Realism and Marxist social insights.[3] In 1945, he was appointed as Secretary, Youth Department, Mar Thoma Church, and married Pennamma in the same year. He attended the World Youth Conference at Oslo in 1947.[4] He was the first Asia Secretary of W. S. C. F. In 1953-54, Thomas spent a year at Union Theological Seminary, New York, for studies. During this period, he attended the assembly of W. C. C. at Evanston as consultant and leader in the Canadian Student Christian Movement Study Course.[5]

---

[3] *Ibid*.14-29.

[4] T. M. Philip, *The Encounter Between Theology and Ideology* (Madras: The CLS, 1986), 9 & 13.

[5] Hielke T. Wolters, *Theology of Prophetic Participation*, 52.

M.M. Thomas was Director, CISRS, from 1962-1976. He edited the Christian weekly, *The Guardian*, from 1964-76. Also, he served as Contributing Editor of the American Christian journal, *Christianity*.[6] He also served as Editor, *Religion and Society*, Bangalore (1962-78), and Chairman, Central Committee, W. C. C. (1968-75).[7] In 1969, his wife died due to cancer.[8] The uncompromising attitude of M.M. Thomas towards human rights violation and political tyranny during the Emergency period is noticeable. When Prime Minister Indira Gandhi proclaimed Emergency in June 1975, Thomas expressed his protest and feelings in several ways. During that period, he actively involved in the struggle for civil and political rights as Chairman of Kerala People's Union for Civil Liberties and Democratic Rights (PUCLDR). He was Joint Secretary and Joint Treasurer of the Detenues Family Distress Relief Fund for the relief of families and prisoners during the Emergency period. He was also visiting professor at some of the universities and seminaries in USA (The Andover Newton School of Theology and Princeton Theological Seminary). He also served the Mar Thoma Church through his membership in Mar Thoma Church Assembly and as Director, Yuhanon Mar Thoma Study Centre, Trivandrum.[9]

M. M. Thomas also served as Chairman, Programme for Social Action (P.S.A.). It is a kind of network of action groups from all over India. He was also the Governor of Nagaland from 9th May 1990 to 2nd April 1992. Thomas was dismissed

---

[6] *Ibid*, 83-85.

[7] Jesudas M. Athyal, ed. *M.M. Thomas, The Man and His Legacy* (Manjadi: The Thiruvalla Ecumenical Charitable Trust and Thiruvalla: CSS, 1997), 100.

[8] *Ibid.*, 15.

[9] Hielke T. Wolters, *Theology of Prophetic Participation*, 121-123.

from the post on two formal charges: firstly, he did not consult the Central Government before approving the dissolution of the State Assembly; and secondly, he was not willing to accept the arguments of Central Government for the suspension of Nagaland Chief Secretary.[10] He founded Thiruvalla Ecumenical Charitable Trust and himself deposited an amount of Rs. 10,00,000 as an endowment for the Trust.[11] He was conferred Honorary Doctorate by the universities of Serampore, Leidon (Netherlands) and Uppsala (Sweden). He was also visiting professor of University of Bochum, West Germany, Southern Methodist University and Texas for interpreting Gandhi for the Modern World, Ecumenism and Plural Society. Dr. M. M. Thomas passed away on 3rd December 1996 at the age of 80, when he was traveling by train from Madras to his native place, Thiruvalla. He was survived by two sons and one daughter.[12]

Major Influences on the Theological Pursuit of M. M. Thomas

M. M. Thomas is a social thinker and theologian. According to David C. Scott, "M. M. Thomas is not only shaping but also being shaped by the world view of his generation."[13] M. M. Thomas' theological articulation was always in relation to the historical situation he encountered.[14] This approach is explained in the preface written by T. M. Philip to

---

[10] *Ibid.*, 151.

[11] Jesudas M. Athyal, *M. M. Thomas, The Man and His Legacy*, 67.

[12] *Ibid.*, 100.

[13] David C. Scott, "A Mirror to M.M. Thomas' Perspective on Inter Religious Studies" in *Christian Witness in Society*, edited by K.C. Abraham (Bangalore : BTE-SSC, 1998), 159.

[14] T. Jacob Thomas, *M.M. Thomas Reader, Selected Texts on Theology, Religion and Society* (Thiruvalla: CSS: 2002), 11.

"M. M. Thomas Reader, Selected Texts on Theology, Religion and Society", edited by T. Jacob Thomas:

> The story of 'my spiritual, theological and ideological pilgrimage' that is how Dr. M. M. Thomas described his lifelong struggle to understand Christian faith seeking its challenging relevance for Asian Revolutionary changes and struggles for social justice and human dignity. Standing at the inter-section between the church and the world Thomas did his Theology. In short, the Gospel message and its relation to the historical situation is key to Thomas' Theology.[15]

It means that his theological assumptions are related to contemporary human issues and that he understood Christian faith has challenging relevance to social transformation. In his theological journey, M. M. Thomas was influenced by his family background, eminent theologians, national leaders and secular ideologies.

In his early life, Thomas was influenced by at least three things in his spiritual and theological development. They are:

> The Mar Thoma church tradition and its characteristic emphasis on liturgy and sacraments, on personal faith and on social responsibility; secondly the personal faith received from his family background; thirdly his involvements in youth movements, particularly, the S. C. M., which helped Thomas to relate his personal faith to his social environment.[16]

It is evident that Thomas was very much influenced by the spiritual atmosphere in his early days. Books such as Weather Head's *Transforming Friendship*, Brother Lawrence's *Practice of the Presence of God* and Baron Von Hugel's *Life of Prayer* played a significant role in his personal meditation. Writers like Canon

---

[15] *Ibid*.

[16] Hielke T. Wolters, *Theology of Prophetic Participation*, 12.

Streeter, A. E. Carvie, W. R. Maltely and William Temple encouraged him to participate in inter-religious dialogue. The work at Bala Bhavan in Trivandrum inspired Thomas to focus on social reality and human personality. By working with street boys, he could understand the meaning of genuine love.[17]

Nehru's thoughts made Thomas aware of the spiritual dimension of corporate life and the structures of culture, society and state in the following way: "India's caste system enslaved one fifth of the people of India as outcastes for several centuries.Nehru though a secular humanist, used to attack the system, not just as irrational. Using religious language, he spoke of 'this demon of caste' which has to be 'exorcised' from the body-politic of India."[18] By quoting Nehru, Thomas shows the need for corporate life that is not controlled by the caste system. His stress on the statement, 'though a secular humanist, Nehru attacked the caste system', reveals that Thomas' main focus was on emphasising the role of Christians in working for a casteless society. Thomas got the 'Concept of New Humanity' from the Indian understanding of Jesus as the Divine Man or the New Adam, the Bearer of New Humanity, the New Creation. He got this understanding from Indian theologians like K. C. Sen, Chenchaiah, Chakkarai and P. D. Devanandan.[19] 'Christian Realism' of Reinhold Neibuhr, 'Biblical Realism' of Hendrik Kraemer, Gandhian concept of society based on 'Varna-Dharma' and Nicolas Berdyaev's idea of 'New Christian Middle Age' tremendously influenced the

---

[17] *Ibid.,* 13-15.

[18] M. M. Thomas, *The Gospel of Forgiveness and Koinonia* (Delhi : ISPCK and Thiruvalla : CSS, 1994), 29.

[19] M. M. Thomas, *Salvation and Humanization* (Madras : The CLS, 1971), 18.

development of Thomas' thinking. Though Thomas was influenced by the ideas of 'Varna-dharma' and 'New Christian Middle Age' for a new organic society, the Brahminic domination in the Indian society and the clericalism in Medieval Europe led him to point out the lack of realism in those concepts.[20] 'Varna Dharma' and clericalism directly or indirectly support the caste system and class structure. Though Varna Dharma creates an organic society where all people do their respective jobs, the condition of low-caste people remains unchanged. So it cannot create a society where all people enjoy equality, justice and freedom. Clericalism makes people submissive to religious ethos and gradually makes them inactive to respond to the violation of human values and freedom.

An important event that stimulated the thinking of M.M. Thomas was the 'Emergency Period of 1975-1977.' It is evident in his famous book, *Response to Tyranny*. Thomas protested against Emergency; he was convinced that:

> Fundamental rights of freedom and justice are, from the Christian point of view, given by God and not by the State, not even by the people. They belong to men and women as spiritual and moral beings. What the state and people have not given, they cannot take away. The State and people can gain their political health by recognizing them, or destroy it by denying them.[21]

The negation of fundamental rights is sin against God since they are given by Him. So human rights violations in religious, social and political areas are to be evaluated in this perspective.

---

[20] Hielke T. Wolters, *Theology of Prophetic Participation*, 26-33.

[21] M. M. Thomas, *Response to Tyranny* (Delhi: Forum for Christian Concern for People's Struggle, 1979), 72.

Gandhism

M.M.Thomas had a high regard for Gandhism. He acknowledged the Christian principle of love in the Gandhian concept of 'Ahimsa.' The Gandhian approach of non-violence and satyagraha influenced Thomas to participate in the national independence struggle.[22] Satyagraha is being observed by political parties, institutions and social action groups for their rights and privileges in contemporary society. Then, what is the relevance of Satyagraha among the people who are deprived of their rights and privileges? M. M. Thomas was attracted to Gandhi because Gandhi "spoke of the spirituality of detachment, 'Nishkama karma', as the basis of his political struggles."[23] Thomas was of the opinion that "the technique of non-violence is the most unique contribution of Gandhi, even those who did not accept it as an absolute ethical creed have realized its importance in the contemporary world, not only as a means of struggle for freedom as Gandhi envisaged it, but also as a realistic ethic of international relation in the face of the nuclear threat and for the fight for justice."[24] Thomas appreciates the Gandhian critique of liberalism. According to him, "It was the merit of Gandhi that he undertook a serious attempt to bring politics and economics under ethical control."[25] Thomas finds that the Gandhian programme of Satyagraha is relevant in the situation where effective constitutional actions are not open.[26]

---

[22] Hielke T. Wolters, *Theology of Prophetic Participation*, 24.

[23] M. M. Thomas, *The Gospel of Forgiveness and Koinonia*, 29.

[24] T. M. Philip, *The Encounter Between Theology and Ideology*, 90.

[25] M.M. Thomas, *Ideological Quest within Christian Commitment* (Madras : The CLS for the CISRS Bangalore, 1983), 240.

[26] *Ibid.*, 250.

M. M. Thomas considered Gandhism as a competing ideology in the national struggle for independence because of its values. But when he approached Gandhism by his framework of theological anthropology built upon Christological foundation, he began to redefine Gandhian ideology.[27] Thomas argued that "Gandhism is particularly important because of its values; however, these values lack strength, since they are based on wrong theological and anthropological pre-suppositions."[28] So Thomas began to re-interpret Gandhian values through its theological and anthropological pre-suppositions. He focused on three values: Ahimsa, Satyagraha and Swadesi.

Thomas did not accept Ahimsa' as a theologically ground concept, but rather as a technique of which the relevance depends on the situation.[29] It means that Gandhian ideology of non-violence cannot be taken as the only possible political technique but one of the techniques. There are many situations where non-violent means are not applicable.[30] It does not mean that violent means of political struggles are applicable in all situations. In a situation where government is passive to respond to the issues or the non-violent protest, people may turn violent. So, in such situations, non-violent means may not be applicable. Non-violent means are not for complete destruction but to show the seriousness of the protest. Regarding the aspect of Satyagraha, Thomas argues that the effectiveness of Satyagraha would depend upon the situation. But Gandhi claimed that it would be effective in all situations.[31]

---

[27] T. M. Philip, *The Encounter Between Theology and Ideology*, 89.

[28] Hielke T. Wolters, *Theology of Prophetic Participation*, 69.

[29] M. M. Thomas, *Ideological Quest within Christian Commitment*, 249.

[30] Hielke T. Wolters, *Theology of Prophetic Participation*, 70.

[31] *Ibid.*, 71.

According to Thomas, "Satyagraha must be considered as effective only in situations where there is still consciousness of universal values and human rights and some awareness of mutual responsibility on that basis."[32] Satyagraha may not be applicable in an autocratic administrative setup where human rights are not protected. In a theocratic state, where religious fundamentalists control power, Satyagraha may not be successful because they prefer religious rules to universal values. Thomas argued that "Gandhi approached 'Swadesi' as a religious belief instead of a relative socio-economic principle. If Swadesi is taken as a relative social principle, it can have great value for Indian economic development."[33] The Swadesi ideology of Gandhi has been interpreted 'religiously' by Hindu fundamentalists. What we need today is the interpretation of 'Swadesi' in a socio-economic perspective to resist multinational companies. So Thomas understands that Gandhian ideas of Satyagraha, Ahimsa and Swadesi are relevant if they can be re-defined in the light of Christian realism.[34] Thomas approached Gandhism as an ideology that is applicable to all aspects of human life. When he evaluated it in the light of Gospel, he came to know that it was not competent enough to respond to social realities. That is why Thomas suggested a re-definition of Gandhism in the light of Christian realism.

Scientific Marxism

M.M. Thomas started his career as a Gandhian, but soon shifted to "Marxian ideology which seems to be capable of providing a better tool for the analysis of society and as a

---

[32] M. M. Thomas, *Ideological Quest within Christian Commitment*, 250.

[33] Hielke T. Wolters, *Theology of Prophetic Participation*, 71.

[34] *Ibid.*, 72.

vehicle for effecting radical changes in Indian society."[35] With the help of Marxian insights, Thomas started his reflection on a theology of society. He said, "The criticism of the Church itself forms part of the criticism of the society" and he did this with the insights gained from Marxian thought.[36] M.M. Thomas views that "Marxism is able to win the confidence of the oppressed because of their realistic approach to power in carrying on the struggles."[37] Marxian ideology has attracted many people to oppose slavery, the caste system and other social evils that prevailed in Kerala society. Its influence on Liberation Theology is noticeable. Since Marxian insights focused on the struggles of poor people who were under economic and political exploitation, it could influence the confidence of the oppressed groups. The concept of New Humanity and Marxian ideology are very much related in the aspects of social justice and human dignity.

The Marxian notion of class interest operating behind social and political forces influenced M.M.Thomas tremendously.[38] Thomas observes that "Neo-orthodoxy of Berdyaev, Neibuhr and Barth provided a framework to accept Marx's scientific interpretation of society and to co-operate with Marxist politics arising from it, and at the same time to reject Marxism as a total interpretation of human reality."[39] The most important criticism of Thomas against Marxism is that "it does not consider the basic contradiction in the human person." For him, 'will to power' is the result of some basic contradictions in human nature.[40]

---

[35] T. M. Philip, *The Encounter Between Theology and Ideology,* 98.

[36] *Ibid.*

[37] M. M. Thomas, *Ideological Quest within Christian Commitment,* 76.

[38] T. M. Philip, *The Encounter Between Theology and Ideology,* 99.

[39] M. M. Thomas, *Ideological Quest within Christian Commitment,* 75.

[40] T. M. Philip, *The Encounter Between Theology and Ideology,* 100.

Thomas was very much influenced by Scientific Marxism, i.e., Marxist interpretation of socio-economic and political forces, which does not claim to be a total interpretation of reality.[41] Because of the influence of Scientific Marxism, he stood for classless society in which democracy is to be upheld in line with Gandhian thought and is to be strengthened by Christian realism.Like Gandhism, Thomas desired to understand Marxism in the light of Christian realism. The classless society that Scientific Marxism upheld can be taken as the meeting point of the New Humanity concept and Scientific Marxism. During the 1940's, Thomas concentrated more on the insights of 'left nationalism', which was represented by congress socialists and Communist Party of India.[42] The Marxian influence can be seen in the 'Aim and Basis' of NCYC founded by M. M. Thomas in 1943. It says "The Council recognizes the struggle between the class which owns and controls the means of production of goods and services necessary to the 'Good Life' and that which class does not so own, as in large measure basic to all other social conflicts in the world today."[43] Though Marxism influenced Thomas to think in line with social changes, he rejected the Marxian view of history. According to him, "Marxism, which began as an ideology of the historical being of man, ended up as a naturalism which reduced history to the inevitable working out of the natural necessity according to the law of dialectical materialism rather than the working out of historical freedom, decision and creativity of man."[44] Thomas gave importance

---

[41] Hielke T. Wolters, *Theology of Prophetic Participation*, 68.

[42] *Ibid.*, 44.

[43] M. M. Thomas, *Ideological Quest within Christian Commitment*, 77.

[44] M. M. Thomas, "Search for a New Humanism as Foundation for the Struggle for a Just Society" in *Political Prospects in India*, edited by Saral K. Chatterji (Madras : The CLS, 1971), 185.

to the creativity of man for the transformation of society. He emphasised human dignity and freedom from all kinds of oppression and exploitation. The problem with Marxian ideology of history is that human being is considered as an object of history, but Thomas considered human being as a subject having freedom, decision and creativity.

Liberal or Social Democracy

Gandhian ideas and disappointment about Communism led Thomas to search for a new ideological position, i.e., Liberal or Social Democracy. He rejected communism because of its violent methods to attain the goal of liberation. For him, the adjective 'liberal' has a positive meaning—'as involving openness to faith at depth.' Social democracy has emerged from parliamentary democracy, socialism and Gandhism. The Indian leaders who represented social democracy are Nehru, Asoka Mehta and Jaya Prakash Narayan.[45] Thomas observes that "Gandhism does not recognize the class struggle which socialism does. Socialism, therefore, goes a step further and seeks to use all non-violent methods (both organized constitutional agitation and peaceful civil disobedience) in the class struggle to attain its ends; thus keeping politics the servant of the truly social revolution."[46] M. M. Thomas was attracted to social democracy because of its rejection of hierarchical socio-cultural stratification in India. He argues for a radical re-definition of ancient Hindu culture to support social democracy and to build India as a modern nation.[47] The main factor that attracted him to socialism was its struggle for justice. By emphasising the need for the re-definition of Hindu culture, Thomas meant an egalitarian culture that is

---

[45] Hielke T. Wolters, *Theology of Prophetic Participation*, 73.

[46] M. M. Thomas, *Ideological Quest within Christian Commitment*, 232.

[47] Hielke T. Wolters, *Theology of Prophetic Participation*, 74.

based on the values of social democracy, such as freedom, equality and justice.

In the socialist line, M. M. Thomas was influenced by Jaya Prakash Narayan's (J.P's) concept of 'lok niti' (power of people). But the 'raj niti' aspect (power of party politics) was rejected by him. Thomas upheld the significance of 'lok niti', which does not make 'raj niti' unnecessary. The 'lok niti' concept of J. P. influenced the working-class people in the 1970s. This time, Thomas developed a political ideology that gave importance not only to the power of people, but also to the necessity of political parties. J. P. and Thomas had different theological or philosophical starting points in their political judgment. Jaya Prakash Narayan's social ethics is based on the religious experience of Vedantic monism, while Thomas starts from the alienation of human being from the self, God and neighbour. The Sarvodaya movement influenced M. M. Thomas by giving an example of community building.[48] This community-building aspect, which promotes the welfare of all, can be seen through the theological formulations of M. M. Thomas.

New Socialism

An ideological uncertainty prevailed in the 1980's. The Congress Party failed to fulfill the needs of the people, and the socialist and leftist parties divided ideologically. They had no clear political ideology in this period. This uncertainty continued even in the early 1990's. This period witnessed the impact of globalisation in all aspects of human life. In this context, Thomas was attracted to New Socialism, which is able to address the present problems created by a wrong concept of modernisation.[49] Globalisation seriously affected the poor

---

[48] *Ibid.* 113-114.

[49] *Ibid.*, 165-166.

people, especially dalits, tribals and other minority groups. In this context, Thomas developed the idea of new socialism. In developing New Socialism, Thomas said:

> Third World has to go beyond the classical capitalist-socialist concept of what has been called the economic man, and take seriously the awakening of Dalits, Tribals, women, cultural minorities and other communities to their separate self-identity and corresponding rights in the body politic not as a super structural reflection of class-reality as Marxism tends to interpret but as independent social realities themselves.[50]

In the context of the exploitation of natural resources by multinational companies, M. M. Thomas related eco-justice to social justice. So, he observes that eco-justice and social justice are inseparable and this inclusive concept of justice serves as the basis for New Socialism. According to M. M. Thomas:

> New Socialism is the renewal of democratic socialism, which involves rethinking on the forms of multinational, political economic structures suitable to check the exploitative aspects of big power and multinational economics and humanize them. It also involves rethinking on the patterns of technological development; so that they may serve the goals of social justice, world peace and integrity of creation.[51]

Neo-socialism is not for supporting exploitative structures but for the protection of social justice and humanisation in the modern developmental process.

Church as New Humanity in Christ

The concept of 'New Humanity in Christ' is a significant portion of the theological discussions of M. M. Thomas. It was

---

[50] M.M. Thomas, *Nagas Towards AD 2000* (Madras : Centre for Research on New International Economic Order, 1992), 209.

[51] Hielke T. Wolters, *Theology of Prophetic Participation*, 167.

formulated during the 1960s, especially in the background of W. C. C Assembly of Uppsala in 1968. The Uppsala assembly discussed the idea of 'New Humanity' based on the Pauline concept of the Risen Christ as the New Man, particularly in section II on "Renewal in Mission." All the heated discussions around the topic in the assembly encouraged Thomas to work out his own theological reflections on the idea of 'New Humanity in Christ.'

The Concept of New Humanity in Christ

M.M. Thomas elaborated the concept of New Humanity in different dimensions of human life. According to him, "The gospel of Resurrection is good news of a new human fellowship, a new community, a New Humanity. Newness of life means not merely the newness of the inner being of man, but renewal also of human relations."[52] Liberation and renewal can be considered as important aspects of New Humanity. It is a fellowship that upholds humanisation and renewal of broken relationships. Reflecting on New Humanity, he quotes Paul that this fellowship in Christ (New Humanity) transcends not only religious divisions, but also all divisions created in society by nature, culture or history.[53] Social and religious barriers, which dehumanise the human community, have no place in this fellowship. Jesus the God Incarnate, the New Adam, is the source of New Humanity. It transcends all divisions created by religion, caste, class, culture, race, nationality, sex, etc. Jesus breaks down every aspect of partition, i.e., between religions (Jews and Gentile), cultures (Greek and Barbarian), classes (bonded and free) and the sexes (male and female). He creates a New Humanity out of twain.[54]

---

[52] M. M. Thomas, *New Creation in Christ* (Delhi: ISPCK, 1976), 4.

[53] *Ibid.*

[54] M. M. Thomas, *The Gospel of Forgiveness and Koinonia*, 18-20.

The message of oneness in Christ is predominant in the mission of New Humanity. "The New Humanity is characterized by the experience of liberating faith and liberating grace transcends the borders of the 'Visible Church'."[55] New Humanity envisages liberation, which encompasses freedom from all kinds of bondage[56] and victimisation. Through the liberating faith and liberating grace, New Humanity offers liberation from all kinds of oppression, exploitation and dehumanisation. The vision of New Humanity is not limited to the visible church, as New Humanity stands for the renewal of the entire humanity.

M.M. Thomas comments that "This new society (New Humanity in Christ) is based on the common acknowledgement of divine forgiveness in Christ and therefore of the need of mutual forgiveness: 'forgiving one another as the Lord has forgiven you'."[57]

God constantly renews humanity and thus makes all things new. He gives a new human nature, a new humanity and a new cosmos.[58] "The new humanity in Christ is being renewed in knowledge after the image of its maker, the distinction of nature, history, culture are not absolutised but transcended in the awareness of solidarity with all mankind and common participation in the New Humanity in Christ."[59]

---

[55] V. Devasahayam, "Search for the Last, the Least and the Lost – Dr. M.M. Thomas' understanding of the Humans, God and the New Humanity" in *Christian Witness in Society* edited by K. C. Abraham (Bangalore: BTE-SSC, 1998), 129.

[56] *Ibid.*

[57] M. M. Thomas, *New Creation in Christ*, 5.

[58] *Ibid.,* 7.

[59] M. M. Thomas, "The Secular Theologies of India and the Secular Meaning of Christ" in *Readings in Indian Christian Theology Vol.I* edited by R. S. Sugirtharajah and Cecil Hargreaves (Delhi : ISPCK, 1993), 98.

The centrality of divine forgiveness releases men and women from the idolatry of communalism of religion, race, nation, class, sex and caste or even ideology, which in alienated conditions, provides spiritual and social security.[60] "The New Humanity which God recreates in Jesus Christ is the basis of a new human solidarity transcending narrow human solidarities based on religion, culture, society or nature."[61] The approach of universal inclusivism is emphasised here. In that light, Thomas brings human solidarity in sin and divine forgiveness as the ultimate criterion for the creation of new community. Human solidarity in sin points to the sinful nature of man that supports the elements of evil forces. The new human solidarity is focused on identification with those who suffer from social disabilities.

It is God's righteous act in Cross that redeems man from his self-righteousness and helps to realise New Humanity, which is created in the image of God.[62] It is the self-righteousness of individuals that creates divisions based on religion, caste, colour, etc., in society. Thomas observes that "New Humanity in Christ is the evidence of the inauguration of Kingdom of God in World history."[63] For him, New Humanity can be or will be realised only when the differences between peoples, groups and classes are broken down in the Christ event in which the sinner is justified.[64] New Humanity

---

[60] T. M. Philip, *The Encounter Between Theology and Ideology : An Exploration into the Communicative Theology of M. M. Thomas*, 131.

[61] *Ibid.*, 130.

[62] M. M. Thomas, *Christava Samuhia Dharmam* [Mal.] (Thiruvalla : The TLC, 1972), 28.

[63] *Ibid.*, 36.

[64] M. M. Thomas, *Man and the Universe of Faiths* (Madras: CISRS-CLS, 1975), 140.

and Kingdom of God uphold the values of justice, equality and peace. Thomas continues to say that "The Crucified and Risen Jesus Christ can be presented as the revealer and bearer of true humanism."[65] The resurrection of Jesus marks the inauguration of a New Humanity in the midst of history.[66] Therefore, Risen Christ is the foundation of freedom and renewal. New Humanity is not only the outcome of the resurrection of Jesus Christ, but also his glorification. Jesus' resurrection and subsequent glorification are the basis of hope. The mission of the Church is to bring that hope to human life.

M. M. Thomas understands New Humanity in the context of inter-faith relations. He says that "New Humanity in Christ is the response to all religions to abolish or at least lower the walls of religious exclusiveness."[67] It transforms other religions and atheistic ideologies and takes new and diverse forms in them.[68] According to M. M. Thomas, "New Humanity in Christ has ability to renew all religions and ideologies in the world."[69] Here New Humanity aims at inter-faith dialogue and relations for the creation of a new society, where there is no narrow divisions based on religion.

M. M. Thomas also explained New Humanity in social dimension. God has bestowed human beings, a New Humanity in Christ. The two important aspects of this new

---

[65] M. M. Thomas, *Some Theological Dialogues*, 97.

[66] M. M. Thomas, *Atmika Sareeram* [Mal.] (Thiruvalla : The CLS, 1978), 7.

[67] T. Jacob Thomas, ed., *M. M. Thomas: Reader, Selected Texts on Theology, Religion and Society*, 149.

[68] M. M. Thomas, *Risking Christ for Christ's Sake* (Geneva: WCC Publications, 1987), 119.

[69] M. M. Thomas, *Parivarthanathinte Daivasasthram* [Mal.] (Thiruvalla : TLC, 1982), 123.

humanity are 'Liberation' from the forces that destroy humanness and 'Reconciliation' with God.[70] "Thus social life based on Christ is the means to reflect the New Humanity in Christ."[71] In our ever-changing society, it is the mission of the Church to actualise New Humanity in Christ through human consciousness and external elements. For that, the Church is called to proclaim and strengthen the witness of New Humanity and to exhort modern human society into that direction.[72] While referring to the social dimension of New Humanity, M. M. Thomas gives much emphasis on the means of self-righteousness, which make love among human beings and justice in the society impossible.[73] That is why he said; "New Humanity is a gift which delivers people from self-righteousness."[74] It implies that New Humanity will be realised if the deliverance from self-righteous is achieved. Since New Humanity renews human relations in socio-cultural areas, it does not renew individuals alone but their societal life wholistically.[75]

According to M. M. Thomas, "the fellowship of the church is sign and sacrament of New Humanity which is given by God in Jesus Christ."[76] Thomas urges "the church to reconsider its form and to become an open community as a sign of New Humanity amidst India's secular and religious life. For, then

---

[70] M. M. Thomas, *Sarva Srushtikkum Aadya Jathan* [Mal.] (Thiruvalla : The CLS., 1977), 8.

[71] *Ibid.*, 93.

[72] M. M. Thomas, *Parivarthanathinte Daivasasthram* [Mal.], 112.

[73] *Ibid.*, 111.

[74] *Ibid.*

[75] M. M. Thomas, *Yesu Christuvil Oru Puthiya Manushian* [Mal.] (Thiruvalla : The CLS, 1983), 44.

[76] M. M. Thomas, *Towards a Theology of Contemporary Ecumenism* (Madras : The CLS, 1978), 1

it can become a powerful force of change and renewal in India's communalistic society"[77] The Church as a sign of New Humanity is the channel of the renewal of humankind. It is the spiritual foundation, the source of judgement, renewal and ultimate fulfillment of the struggles of people today.[78] As a sign of New Humanity in Christ, the Church is called to involve in the struggles of humankind for human dignity and just society. New Humanity, as a source of renewal, is for the ultimate humanization of entire humanity."[79] The Risen Jesus is the guarantee and head of that New Humanity. He offers total liberation and ultimate humanization.[80]

Finally, M. M. Thomas interprets New Humanity as new creation in Christ. "The core of the gospel is the good news of the New Humanity, the new creation in Christ."[81] He opines that "in our day and age, when men and women are filled with the vision of New Humanity and are struggling to achieve a fuller and richer human life, this message of Jesus Christ as the foundation and mediator of a New Humanity is most relevant."[82]

M. M. Thomas understands the New Creation (New Humanity) in three aspects. Firstly, in Christ, a new human nature is offered, a renewal of our inner-being.[83] This renewal includes the body as a part of human personality. In the Risen

---

[77] Hielke T. Wolters, *Theology of Prophetic Participation*, 237.

[78] M. M. Thomas, *Salvation and Humanization* (Madras: the CLS, 1971), P.4.

[79] *Ibid.*, 19.

[80] M. M. Thomas, *Towards a Theology of Contemporary Ecumenism*, P.316.

[81] M. M. Thomas, *New Creation in Christ*, P.78.

[82] *Ibid.*

[83] *Ibid.*, 3.

Christ, we receive a total new being.[84] Secondly, "the gospel of Resurrection is the good news of a new human fellowship, a new community, a New Humanity."[85] This new human fellowship is not merely limited to the Church alone but transforms the social relations and thus brings a reality of new society.[86] Thirdly, "Christ brings renewal not only to the inner-being of man, not only to the human relations in the society, but also to the whole cosmos – 'all things' in heaven and earth."[87] In short, New Humanity in Christ witnesses a renewal of the whole cosmos, a new human fellowship, a richer human life and total liberation from destructive elements.

Biblical Background of New Humanity

M. M. Thomas uses different biblical passages to develop his concept of New Humanity. He sees the renewal of life and world has been achieved through Jesus Christ. Thomas says that "in the resurrection of Jesus, God not only raises Jesus from the dead, but out of nothing, He also brings into being, in the Risen Christ, a new world, a new creation."[88] This is the good news for humanity. The Gospel of New Humanity in Christ brings total transformation and liberation in human life.

M. M. Thomas refers to New Testament passages such as 2 Corinthians 5:17-19, Colossians 3:10-13, Ephesians 4:22-24, Revelation 21:5 etc. 2 Corinthians 5:17-19 (R. S. V.) says, "Therefore, if anyone is in Christ, he is a new creation; the old has passed away, behold, the new has come. All this is from

---

[84] Hielke T. Wolters, *Theology of Prophetic Participation*, 98.

[85] M. M. Thomas, *New Creation in Christ*, P.4.

[86] *Ibid.*, 5.

[87] *Ibid.*, 6.

[88] *Ibid.*

God, who through Christ reconciled us to himself and gave us the ministry of reconciliation; that is, in Christ God was renewing the world to himself, not counting their trespasses against them, and intrusting to us the message of reconciliation." Thomas explains that "in Christ, there is the offer of a new human nature, a renewal of our inner-being. Therefore one is joined to Christ, he is a new being, the old is gone, the new has come."[89] Referring to 2 Cori. 5:17, he said that "in history, there is a movement of renewal of all things taking place in Jesus Christ and through Him. This movement totally changes history in all its aspects."[90] It implies that Jesus is the source of ultimate humanisation. He quotes Ephesians 4:22-24 (R. S. V.) to discuss this theme, "Put off your old nature which belongs to your former manner of life and is corrupt through deceitful lusts, and be renewed in the spirit of your minds, and put on the new nature, created after the likeness of God in true righteousness and holiness." Based on the above passage, Thomas views that "Jesus Christ became the good news of a New Humanity, a new human dignity, the source of a new society"[91]

Thomas again quotes Colossians 3:10-13 (R. S. V) to substantiate his idea of New Humanity that, "have put on the new nature, which is being renewed in knowledge after the image of its creator. Here, there cannot be Greek and Jew, circumcised and uncircumcised, barbarian, scythian, slave, free man, but Christ is all and in all." Here Paul speaks of the gospel as the renewal of human nature and human relations at once. Terms such as 'the new self', 'the new being', 'the

---

[89] Ibid.,3.

[90] Hielke T. Wolters, *Theology of Prophetic Participation*, 97.

[91] M. M. Thomas, *Church and Human Community* (Delhi: ISPCK, 1985), 43.

new humanity', or 'the new nature' in different translations speak of a renewal of human life and relations in their totality. Thomas finds out three aspects of the corporate character of the New being or New Humanity from this passage. Firstly, "there is a new quality of unity transcending and transforming life and relations in communities based on nature, culture or nation, on law or religion. Secondly, there is a fellowship of mutual forgiveness, which is the corporate response of faith to the divine forgiveness on which alone men and women have standing ground. Thirdly, the point of entry into the whole realm of redemption is divine forgiveness offered in Christ to men and women."[92] Father God creates a New Humanity and a new humanness in Jesus Christ as a fruit of kingdom. The Holy Spirit is the means of the creation of this New Humanity on earth.[93] The New Humanity, which is created by God in Christ, is characterised by unity, mutual forgiveness and redemption through divine forgiveness.

Thomas, along with three aspects of New Being in Christ, depicts a new communion of the spirit, which is related to New Humanity in Christ. "Through Jesus Christ a new communion of the spirit, based on mutual forgiveness and gratitude to the Divine forgiveness received in Christ, building up tissues of love comes into being among the communities of the world, producing spiritual ferment of their renewal and humanization"[94] The new communion of the spirit renews people even outside the Church. It abolishes narrow human solidarities based on religion and culture. Thomas draws out

---

[92] M. M. Thomas, *The Gospel of Forgiveness and Koinonia*, 2-3.

[93] M. M. Thomas, *Christava Samuhia Dharmam* ,33.

[94] M. M. Thomas, "The Secular Ideologies of India and the Secular meaning of Christ' in *Readings in Indian Christian Theology* Vol.1, edited by R.S. Sugirtharajah and Cecil Hargreaves, 98.

an eschatological and ecological dimension of New Humanity from Revelation 21:5 (R. S. V.): "And he sat upon the throne said, 'Behold I make all things new.'" Jesus Christ is the New man through whom a New Humanity is created. He bears the movement of spirit leading to the ultimate renewal of man and nature and to the final consummation of the kingdom. Through Him, a new cosmos is being emerged.[95] Renewal of nature envisages a new cosmos, which is not being exploited by human being for his or her vested interests.

New Humanity in the Indian Theological Discussion

Pandippedi Chenchiah, P. D. Devanandan and Paulos Mar Gregorios have discussed the concept of New Humanity in their theological discussions. P. Chenchiah saw, "the fact of Christ as the birth of a new order of creation; as the emergence of a new life, not bound by karma, not tainted by sin and not humbled by death, and as the manifestation of the first fruits of a new race of the Sons of God in creative process."[96] He conceives, "incarnation as God assuming manhood with a view to create the New Humanity and the new cosmos in His image."[97] Therefore he said, "Jesus is the 'Adhipurusha' of the new creation"[98] For him, Christ is the 'True man', 'the New man' and the Lord and Master of a new creative branch of Cosmos. Thus, Jesus builds the new life order of Kingdom of God through the Holy Spirit.[99] Chenchiah understands

---

[95] M. M. Thomas, *Man and the Universe of Faiths*, P.129.

[96] M. M. Thomas and P.T. Thomas, *Towards an Indian Christian Theology* (Thiruvalla: The New Day Publications of India, 1992), 155.

[97] *Ibid.*

[98] R. H. S. Boyd, *An Introduction to Indian Christian Theology* (Delhi: ISPCK, 2004), 150.

[99] *Ibid.*, 145.

"salvation as a movement towards a new human being, society and cosmos."[100]

Paul Devanandan defined the Gospel as "the gift of a New Humanity, a New creation in Christ and the church's role as that of bearing witness to it through active participation in the struggle for a new society and through a life of spiritual dialogue with the religious and secular faiths is the meaning and basis of being human."[101] In this sense, he says, "Church is the 'sign' of the New creation in Christ, a special sign among other 'signs'"[102] Devanandan understands 'the New Creation' in personal, social and cosmic dimensions.[103]

Paulos Mar Gregorios defined the New Humanity as identification with humanity and he says that "man cannot be a man if he does not identify with the whole of mankind and this is the New Humanity in Jesus Christ."[104] M. M. Thomas related the concept of New Humanity in Christ with the Church. He articulated that the Church is a sign and sacrament of New Humanity that is created by God in Christ. So, the mission of the Church is to bring renewal and transformation in all aspects of human life.

New Humanity and Church

M.M. Thomas views that "church is the foretaste and prophetic sign of the New Humanity created in Christ. The church must

---

[100] M. M. Thomas and P. T. Thomas, *Towards an Indian Christian Theology*, 156.

[101] *Ibid.*, 189.

[102] *Ibid.*, 190.

[103] *Ibid.*

[104] M. Stephen, *A Christian Theology in the Indian Context* (Delhi: ISPCK, 2001), 73.

be present wherever renewal of humanity takes place."[105] M. M. Thomas uses several terms to refer to the Church as the manifestation of the new reality, such as Koinonia, New humanity in Christ, Christ-centered fellowship of faith and Christ-centered secular fellowship. "The Gospel that the church is called to proclaim is a powerful force to bring into actualization of New Humanity."[106] The actualisation of New Humanity focuses inside and outside the Church. The Christian ethics in this world is renewing the life and the world based on the faith in Cross. The main duty of the Church is to transform world communities based on brotherhood and thus becomes the explicit means of New Humanity.[107] Thomas interprets redemption in relation to New Humanity by citing an example of the primitive church. "The primitive church, in the light of the Easter and Pentecostal experiences which gave it birth, identified the crucified Jesus with the expected Messiah. It interpreted the redemptive purpose in history in terms of the New Cruciform Humanity of Jesus Christ. Jesus is the New Man through whom a New Humanity is created after the image of God (Col. 3:10)."[108]

Thomas understands that the Church is the foretaste of a new society and fellowship. So he writes: "The church ought to become the foretaste of a new society and its social fellowship in Christ, the source of a permanent revolutionary ferment."[109] He further adds that "the church cannot be the sign of the New Humanity unless…the church itself is concerned with active participation in the struggle for secular

---

[105] M. M. Thomas, *Gospel of Forgiveness and Koinonia*, 44.

[106] K. C. Abraham, *Christian Witness in Society* (Bangalore: BTE-SCC, 1998), 125.

[107] M. M. Thomas, *Christava Samuhia Dharmam*, 46.

[108] M. M. Thomas, *Man and Universe of Faiths*, 129.

[109] M. M. Thomas, *New Creation in Christ*, 46.

fellowship on a Christ-centered basis."[110] The New Humanity in Christ not only renews the human life inside the Church but also outside the Church. As a sign of New Humanity, the Church is to discern the new creation and to enter into the struggle for a new society.[111] In this context, M. M. Thomas observes that the divine commission of the Church is to witness the Gospel, which renews all world communities in Christ[112] Since New Humanity stands for the humanisation of all world communities, secular human fellowship helps the Church to witness the Gospel of New Humanity.

Thomas identifies New Humanity in two areas: The struggles of society for a secular human fellowship and identification with adherents of other faiths. As a sign of New Humanity, the Church is responsible for getting involved in these two areas.[113] The secular human fellowship and interfaith relations are helpful for the Church to participate in the struggles of people in society. M. M. Thomas understands people's awakening for their rights in relation to the aspect of New Humanity. He observes that "people's awakening everywhere to the dignity of self-hood and to their right to participate in centers of power and their right to bread and life and the struggles for development must be seen within the context of the New Humanity in Christ."[114] In the situation of people's awakening for new society, he clarifies that the mission of the Church is to "let the spirit of God renew and

---

[110] M. M. Thomas, *Some Theological Dialogues*, 114.

[111] T. Jacob Thomas, *M.M. Thomas Reader, Selected Texts on Theology, Religion and Society*, 150.

[112] M. M. Thomas, *Yesuvil Oru Puthiya Manushyan*, 48.

[113] G. R. Smith, "The Ecclesiology of M.M.Thomas," *The SATHRI Journal* Issue No. 2 (1993): 34.

[114] M. M. Thomas, *Towards a Theology of Contemporary Ecumenism*,.216.

reconstruct that world in the pattern of the New Humanity in Christ."[115] While referring to the struggles of people for fuller and richer human life, i.e., the characteristic of New Humanity, Thomas evaluated the role of the Church that it should relate to contemporary secular and religious movements that express man's search for richer and fuller human life.[116] Thomas writes:

> It was the promise of humanization inherent in the gospel of salvation that led to the influx of the oppressed to the church. It was the promise in Christ's salvation of a richer and fuller human life for all men in society and of a new community of freedom and love that attracted some of the intellectuals of the privileged classes of India and brought them to acknowledge Christ as their Lord and God.[117]

M. M. Thomas relates the Church and New Humanity by saying that Christian witness and service should be based on the values of New Humanity, such as universal humanity, unity, equality and mutual love.[118] Since the Church is the visible sign of New Humanity, it should proclaim the Crucified and Risen Lord as the only basis for true humanism.[119] Thomas emphasised the mission of the Church with regard to New Humanity in Christ in this way: "Church consists of members drawn from the various traditional groups and has been built into one community of Divine and human forgiveness, that church can be a channel of the same spirit of forgiveness and reconciliation."[120] He further says that:

---

[115] M. M. Thomas, *Religion and Revolt of the Oppressed* (Delhi: ISPCK, 1981),17.

[116] M. M. Thomas, *Salvation and Humanization*, 4.

[117] *Ibid.*, 14.

[118] M. M. Thomas, *Bharathathil Christava Sabhakalude Samuhika Dharmam* (Thiruvalla: The TLC, 1985), 125.

[119] M. M. Thomas, *Towards a Theology of Contemporary Ecumenism*, 33.

[120] *Ibid.*, 116.

> The mission of the church is to be present within the creative liberation movements of our time which the gospel of Christ itself has helped to take shape, and so to participate in them as to be able to communicate the genuine gospel of liberation–from the vicious circle of sin and alienation, law and self-righteousness, frustration and death into New realm of Christ's New Humanity where there is forgiveness and reconciliation, grace and justification, renewal and eternal life.[121]

In this sense, the Church is called to witness the new life in Christ and to become sign and sacrament of New Humanity.[122] In order to witness the new life in Christ, the Church should be transformed into an atmosphere where the values of New Humanity are being experienced.

Features of New Humanity

M. M. Thomas has highlighted the features of New Humanity in his writings. Let us consider the important ones.

Forgiveness

According to M. M. Thomas, "New Humanity is based on the common acknowledgement of divine forgiveness in Christ and therefore of the need of mutual forgiveness."[123] Cross is the means of divine forgiveness and the creation of a community of forgiven sinners can be considered as the foretaste of New Humanity.[124] M.M.Thomas conceives the aspect of forgiveness

---

[121] *Ibid.*, 184.

[122] V. Devasahayam, "Search for the Last, the Least and the Lost," in *M.M. Thomas, The Man and His Legacy* edited by Jesudas M. Athyal, (Thiruvalla : The Thiruvalla Ecumenical Charitable Trust, in association with CSS, 1997), 52.

[123] M. M. Thomas, *New Creation in Christ*, 5.

[124] *Ibid.*, 20.

in a larger context that "the Gospel of Divine forgiveness offered in the Crucified and Risen Jesus Christ .... gives him or her, a realization of solidarity with all men and women before God, both in sin and in divine forgiveness and opens up the vision and power of a new human fellowship and a New Humanity in Christ."[125] He says that the centre and base of New Humanity is forgiveness in and outside the Church.[126] For M. M. Thomas, New Humanity is a true human community and he said; "True human community is the community of forgiven sinners. Love has ceased to be a law or an idea; in grateful response to the forgiveness of Christ through His death, it becomes a spontaneous fact."[127] In short, the realm of Christ's New Humanity is where there is divine forgiveness and mutual human forgiveness.

Reconciliation

Thomas observes that, "reconciliation is inherent in the act of God who in Jesus Christ has created a new human nature, a new humanity, in which Christ is all and in all, uniting in Himself Greek or Jew, Barbarian and civilized, free man and slave, man and woman, breaking down all walls of partition."[128] So reconciliation is an essential element of New Humanity because New Humanity renews the broken relationships in all dimensions. New Humanity is a reality that destroys all divisions based on religion, community and moral values. It also breaks all walls of partition based on wealth. Reconciliation is not limited to the Church alone; it

---

[125] M. M. Thomas, *The Gospel of Forgiveness and Koinonia*, 1-2.

[126] M. M. Thomas, *Sarva Srushtikkum Aadya Jathan*, 17.

[127] M. M. Thomas, *Towards A Theology of Contemporary Ecumenism*, 35.

[128] M. M. Thomas, New Creation in Christ, 57.

relates to co-operation with people of other faiths in the struggle for a new society. Therefore, Thomas says, "The New Humanity of God's creation in Christ is renewing human life even outside the church."[129]

Abolition of Religious Exclusiveness

M. M. Thomas says:

> The church's witness to Christ consists in entering into partnership with men of other religions and secular faiths in the struggle for a secular Koinonia, learning from them at some points, and correcting them at others, and at the same time pointing to Jesus Christ as the source, criterion and goal of New Humanity they seek.[130]

It implies that New Humanity in Christ breaks down all walls of separation and transforms other religions and ideologies. It has the ability to renew human life even outside the Church. M. M. Thomas suggests that in order to abolish narrow religious exclusiveness, the Church should be able to realise liberating faith and grace outside the Church. For him, "Liberating Faith and Grace, which are the marks of New Humanity in Christ, are present and can be discerned anywhere outside the church. The realities of Faith and Grace outside the church to which the church must open itself if it is to be the church, the nucleus of the New Humanity."[131] The abolition of religious exclusiveness, a feature of New Humanity, points to the abolishing or at least lowering the walls of religious exclusiveness as a part of common response of all religions to the New Humanity in Christ. It is the mission of the Church to discern the possibility of new creation, and

---

[129] M. M. Thomas, *The Gospel of Divine Forgiveness and Koinonia*, 10

[130] M. M. Thomas, *New Creation in Christ*, 47-48.

[131] M. M. Thomas, *Some Theological Dialogues*, 113.

to enter into partnership with people of other religions in the struggle for a new society.[132]

Koinonia in Christ

Koinonia in Christ is an important aspect of New Humanity. M. M. Thomas understands this koinonia at three levels: Koinonia of the eucharistic community of the Church, a larger koinonia of dialogue among people of other faiths and a koinonia of people who involve in the power struggle for new societies.[133] Koinonia acknowledges the diversity of culture, caste, class, ideologies, religions, etc.[134] Thomas holds that, "the reality of the fellowship in Christ's New Humanity is present in active life and thought of men of other religions and secular faiths."[135] For M. M. Thomas, Koinonia in Christ means transcending all communal solidarities and caste outlook of the traditional Indian society. That will help the Church to create an inclusive fellowship of the New Humanity in Christ.[136]

New Human Solidarity

It means the expression of our solidarity with the New Humanity in Christ by transcending all communal or caste solidarities.[137] New Human Solidarity implies the liberation

---

[132] T. Jacob Thomas. ed., *M. M. Thomas Reader, Selected Texts on Theology, Religion and Society*, 149-150.

[133] M. M. Thomas, *Risking Christ for Christ's Sake*, (Geneva: WCC Publications, 1987), 119.

[134] M. M. Thomas, *A Diaconal Approach to Indian Ecclesiology*, 67.

[135] M. M. Thomas, *New Creation in Christ*, 46.

[136] T. M. Philip, *The Encounter Between Theology and Ideology*, 87.

[137] M. M. Thomas, "The Church–The Fellowship of the Baptised and the Unbaptised" in *Liberating Witness* edited by Prasanna Kumari (Madras: The Gurukul Lutheran Theological College and Research Institute, 1995), 15.

from the bondage of communalism of religion, race, nation, caste, sex and even ideology, for the formation of new society.[138] Since "New Humanity is being renewed in the knowledge after the image of its maker, the distinction of nature, history, culture and religion are not abolished but transcended in the awareness of solidarity with all mankind and common participation in the New Humanity in Christ."[139] This human solidarity is not only for transcending all communal barriers, but also for the participation in the struggles of common people for social justice and equality.

Diakonia

M. M. Thomas understands diakonia in the light of New Humanity. For him, this diakonia has two aspects: Firstly, the affirmation of solidarity with the victims of the present process of modernisation, especially the dalits, the tribals, the fisher folk, the women and the urban slum dwellers, in their suffering and struggle for social justice and eco-justice. Secondly, the participation in the exploration of an alternative post-modern pattern of development and a more holistic civil culture.[140]

Ecumenism

Thomas holds that Christian ecumenism can be regarded as the ground and pillar of New Humanity. He writes: "Christian Ecumenism has truth and meaning only as it becomes the ground and pillar of a New humanism which can provide the framework of understanding and critical participation in the revolution of our time."[141] Christian ecumenism is an

---

[138] T. M. Philip, *The Encounter Between Theology and Ideology*, 131.

[139] *Ibid.*

[140] M. M. Thomas, *A Diaconal Approach to Indian Ecclesiology*, 40.

[141] M. M. Thomas, *Towards A Theology of Contemporary Ecumenism*, 164.

important aspect of New Humanity because "church's witness to fellowship in Christ is realized as a sacramental reality in the religious life of the church around the Bible and the Lord's table."[142] Since the fellowship in Christ is a sacramental reality, it denotes the need of an ecumenical atmosphere among church denominations for the emergence of a new humanity within the ecclesiastical context. Thus, "in the sacramental fellowship of the church a new reality, a new humanity, is emerging."[143] Since New Humanity transcends all divisions, the Church as a sign of New Humanity should develop an ecumenical atmosphere among different denominations.[144]

New Humanity: A Means of Revolution

According to M. M. Thomas, "New Humanity transforms the society of individuals and stands as a model and message of community life based on universal love. It also makes changes in existing social elements. Thus New Humanity is a means of revolution for transformation."[145] The humanity that is referred to here is not a humanity based on selfishness, rather a humanity based on divine love.[146] He claims that "Jesus is at work in the revolution as victor over these evil powers through His Cross and Resurrection and His Kingdom and His New Humanity."[147] The promise of Christ for a richer human life for humanity will be fulfilled only if the revolution receives within it, Christ's Gospel of redemption and the New

---

[142] M. M. Thomas, *New Creation in Christ*, 43.

[143] *Ibid.*, 45.

[144] M. M. Thomas, *The Gospel of Forgiveness and Koinonia*, 20.

[145] M. M. Thomas, *Sarva Srushtikkum Aadya Jathan*, 132.

[146] *Ibid.*, 134.

[147] M. M. Thomas, *Towards a Theology of Contemporary Ecumenism*, 35.

creation of which the Church is witness.[148] In fact, New Humanity is a means of revolution in which the Church is the main participant in the revolution for transformation.

Universality of New Humanity

New Humanity in Christ transforms human life as a whole. This New Humanity is a revolutionary force that breaks down the walls of separation and makes the whole humanity a universal family. M. M. Thomas maintains that the exclusive mindset of communal, caste and national elements acts as a strengthening force for the existing walls of separation. But in the universality of New Humanity in Christ, individuals and societies open their doors for mutual interaction and unity. As a result, a brotherhood based on humanness is formed in world communities. In this sense, New Humanity is an instrument of transformation that aims only at Universal humanity in social history.[149]

M. M. Thomas was a lay theologian and social thinker. He interpreted Gospel in the context of the socio-political changes of his time. He tried to bring out the challenging relevance of Gospel in the struggle for social justice and human dignity. His theological outlook was influenced by secular ideologies, like Gandhism and Marxism; Neo-Orthodox theologians, like Karl Barth, Reinhold Niebuhr and Nicolas Berdyaev; Social Action Programmes; and his family background.

New Humanity can be summarised as a humanity that is created by God in Christ. It has various dimensions in which renewal of human life and whole cosmos is the main focus.

---

[148] *Ibid.*, 69.

[149] M. M. Thomas, *Sarva Srushtikkum Aadya Jathan*, 21-24.

The Church, the channel of renewal, is regarded as the sign and sacrament of New Humanity in Christ. This New Humanity is characterised by forgiveness, reconciliation, koinonia, diakonia, new human solidarity, abolition of religious exclusiveness, etc. Thomas refers to biblical passages to elaborate this concept and concludes that Christ is the source of ultimate humanisation and renewal of society. As a sign of New Humanity in Christ, the Church is called to transform world communities in the context of religious fundamentalism, human rights violation and exploitation of nature in today's society. The New Humanity in Christ breaks down all barriers of religious and social ethos and creates a new society that upholds justice, equality, freedom, etc.

Chapter 4

Church as New Humanity in Christ: An Intentional Engagement with People

The concept of New Humanity in Christ is a widely discussed idea in Indian Christian thinking. Many theologians have developed this concept in various dimensions. But M. M. Thomas approached this idea in relation to the mission of the Church in the multi-religious context. He said that the Church is the sign and sacrament of New Humanity in Christ and is called to respond to human issues in society to create a new human community. But, by and large, the Church has forgotten its vocation and failed to get involved in the issues faced by people in today's society.

A Community for Struggle

M. M. Thomas understood the Church in terms of New Humanity in the context of class-caste discrimination, injustice and inequality. From his concept of New Humanity, we may understand that the Church is the paradigm or sign of New Humanity, which stands for social justice, human dignity and egalitarian society. It means that the Church should stand for just cause irrespective of its advantages or disadvantages. But very often, the Church has been failing to carry out the vision and mission of New Humanity for the transformation of society in the context of discrimination and dehumanisation. Human dignity and social justice are the two aspects that Thomas gives emphasis to in the concept of New Humanity in social context.[1] Today's human society, which is gripped by consumerism and globalisation, is not different from that of Thomas' societal background, which is characterised by human issues of injustice, human rights violation, corruption, caste-polarisation, etc. In this situation, as a sign and sacrament of New Humanity, how and to what extent the Church is accountable to respond to social realities or issues in contemporary society is briefly discussed in line with the concept of New Humanity in this chapter.

In the context of struggle for human dignity, M. M. Thomas explains the mission of the Church in terms of New Humanity. He says that "mission of the church should be seen within the context of the Christian solidarity with the poor, in their struggle for human rights and social justice."[2] God created human beings with equal dignity and value. So the violation and negation of that dignity is contrary to divine will and purpose. But the idea of New Humanity in Christ protects the dignity of selfhood of all sections of people in society. That is why M.M. Thomas said, "The people's awakening everywhere to the dignity of selfhood and to their right to participate in centres of power and their right to bread and life and the struggles for development must be seen within

---

[1] M. M. Thomas, *Religion and the Revolt of the Oppressed* (Delhi: ISPCK, 1981), 42.

[2] M. M. Thomas, *New Creation in Christ* (Delhi: ISPCK, 1985), 40.

the context of the New Humanity in Christ."³ Here the Church has the duty to be identified with the people who struggle to recognise their human dignity.

M.M. Thomas categorically says that, "there can be no authentic theology except within responsible encounter with the contemporary world in the name of the dignity of Humanity."⁴ Contextual theologies of the Third World and Latin America are examples of this view. Since present social scenario gives less priority to uphold the dignity of the poor sections in society, the Church as a sign of New Humanity is called to be the foundation of renewal and struggle for human dignity.

According to M.M. Thomas, "The Christian concern for social justice may be defined as the faith response to God's loving and righteous purpose for the world as revealed in the life, death and resurrection of Jesus Christ. It is the faith in Christ as the spiritual motivation for the struggle for justice." ⁵ So, the Church as a community of faith should identify itself with the suffering and hopes of the poor and the oppressed in Indian society. ⁶

In order to foster the hopes of suffering and oppressed groups, M.M. Thomas suggests that the Church should participate in building the awareness of the people of their

---

³ M. M. Thomas, *Towards a Theology of Contemporary Ecumenism* (Madras: The CLS, 1978), 216.

⁴ M. M. Thomas, "Spirituality for Combat" *NCCR Vol XCVI/No.1* (Jan., 1976) : 48.

⁵ M. M. Thomas, *Faith and Ideology in the Struggle for Justice* (Bombay: BUILD, 1987), 3.

⁶ M. M. Thomas, *Revolution in India and Christian Humanism* (Delhi: Forum for Christian Concern for People' s Struggle, 1978), 14.

rights, in speaking truth to dehumanising power in the name of God's justice, in co-operation with other social action groups.[7] Social Action Groups mean the organisations that stand for social justice, equality and freedom. Without the co-operation of these social movements, the Church may not be able to realise its mission of social transformation. With regard to social movements, the mission of the Church is to encourage them in the light of Gospel and to protest against unjust activities and violence in society along with them.[8]

In discussing an ideology of struggle for justice, M.M. Thomas understands two aspects of the meaning of justice:

> They are the objective and the subjective dimensions of justice. The objective dimension is concerned with the changing of institutions of society in which monopoly of economic, political or cultural power in the hands of the few makes possible exploitation and oppression of many. The subjective dimension deals with the development of consciousness of the oppressed people, so that they themselves see the reality of their situation and take the responsibility for changing it and creating new structures and institutions.[9]

According to M.M. Thomas, the Church as a sign of New Humanity "is a fellowship in Christ for building a community on a new basis, where people are in revolt against inequality based on caste, class and race and against paternalism of all kinds."[10] This fellowship not only transcends divisions of

---

[7] *Ibid.*

[8] M. M. Thomas, *Vimochakanaya Daivam* (Thiruvalla: The CLS, 1985), 59.

[9] M. M. Thomas, *Faith and Ideology in the Struggle for Justice*, 31.

[10] M. M. Thomas, *New Creation in Christ*, 76.

caste, class and sex, but also becomes the basis of human unity and dignity.[11] M.M. Thomas continues to say that, "if the church is truly the church in unity and fellowship, it will become a prophetic critique of all social relations and idolatry of caste, class, race or nation, etc." [12] But the present Church is not being motivated into genuine fellowship of New Humanity because of separatism, individualism, caste-consciousness, money-oriented values, etc. So the Church is not able to create a spiritual ferment in it for social transformation and for producing a casteless society. The relevant question is, Like the Marxian ideology of classless society, is the casteless vision of New Humanity possible or not? In relation to the genuine fellowship of New Humanity in Christ, M.M. Thomas explains the social mission of the Church in this way: "First, the spirituality of suffering and service and discipleship of solidarity with victims; secondly, a movement towards prophetic theology and from there to the political theology."[13] The social mission envisages social equality, cultural freedom, spiritual renewal and struggle for bread and against oppressive systems.

M.M. Thomas sees the Church, the sign of New Humanity, in terms of secular fellowship that stands for the struggles of liberation. He believes that, "the church cannot be the sign of the New Humanity unless it is present at this point in the area of the struggle of societies for a secular human fellowship discerning the reality of the New Humanity which is there."[14]

---

[11] M. M. Thomas, *Gospel of Forgiveness and Koinonia* (Delhi: ISPCK and Thiruvalla: CSS, 1994), 15.

[12] *Ibid.*

[13] M. M. Thomas, "Theological Aspects of the Relationship between Social Action Groups and Churches" *Religion and Society Vol. XXXI No.2* (June 1984): 21.

[14] M. M. Thomas, *Some Theological Dialogues* (Madras : The CLS, 1977), 114.

This secular human fellowship does not give up the Christ centredness of faith. It is for the Church one of the means to carry out its social mission. By elaborating secular human fellowship, Thomas views that the "church must involve in the issues of social justice and decide what are the legitimate means of self-defense of the poor in such situations against apparently peaceful but very violent social institutions like caste and landlordism."[15] He suggests that the Church must involve herself with others outside the Church in creating the ideologies that are informed by Christian insights for helping the people in their struggle for social justice and human dignity. But the disturbing fact is that the present ecclesiastical scenario has been moulded to avoid conflict and not to disturb the calm of ongoing life. So the Church does not raise voice against injustice and inequality in society. Today's Church is not ready to join hands with secular groups for awakening the poor and fighting with the poor for social justice.

M.M. Thomas relates social justice with divine righteousness. He says that "human ideals of social justice are the ghost of divine righteousness. This means that social justice is creative only if it indicates or points towards divine righteousness."[16] So a true Christian congregation is the most effective prophetic witness to divine righteousness in society. While witnessing to divine righteousness, it is the responsibility of the Church to proclaim the basic rights of people in society, which no individual or government can disregard or negate. The Christian community is called to safeguard the basic rights and to become prophetic witness

---

[15] M. M. Thomas, *Religion and the Revolt of the Oppressed*, P.52.

[16] Hielke T. Wolters, *Theology of Prophetic Participation* (Delhi: ISPCK and Bangalore: UTC, 1996), 60.

where self-righteous forces are at work.[17] Here the focus is on basic human rights, which are given by God. Since these rights are God-given rights, no one can take them or destroy them. Divine righteousness can be considered as the protection of underprivileged classes' rights and privileges. In the context of the agony of the oppressed, can the Church become a channel of prophetic witness to divine righteousness in the present time? Thomas argues that apart from the task of prophetic witness, the Church has also the task of critical participation. He defined critical participation in this way: "Critical participation should be in terms of the revitalization of values. It means traditional values have to be re-interpreted and redefined in the light of what is understood as the Christian truth in order to revitalize them for the building up of a humane society."[18]

The social dimension of the concept of New Humanity and the social mission of the Church are relevant in the present social context. Money has become the pre-dominant deciding factor in today's societal life. Human dignity and values are being questioned. Corruption distorts the value of justice and righteousness. Directly or indirectly, communal and caste feelings distort the whole fabric of society, and oppressed groups become more oppressed and marginalised. Consumerist lifestyle and culture lead people to accumulate more money and finally lead to corruption and denial of justice to poor people. Though globalisation brings creativity and speedy development in production, it provides benefits to economically influential groups. It reduces unskilled traditional job opportunities and creates unemployment in different sectors of economy. The arrival of multinational

---

[17] M. M. Thomas, *Ideological Quest within Christian Commitment* (Madras: The CLS, 1983), 224-225.

[18] Hielke T. Wolters, *Theology of Prophetic Participation*, 63.

companies in the market affects the employment opportunities of common people in different areas. The Church cannot keep away from responding positively to today's social issues. As a sign and sacrament of New Humanity, the Church very often has failed to respond to social problems effectively. As M.M. Thomas articulated, the Church cannot be the sign of New Humanity, if it does not participate in the struggles of society. In short, the Church is for social transformation and for the realisation of the hopes of those who are deprived of dignity, equality, freedom and justice.

A Community of Prophetic Voice

The concept of New Humanity has another dimension, i.e., political. It promotes the active participation of the Church in politics by leaving communal interests. But today's problem is that the Church gives less importance to the political struggles of less fortunate groups of people like Adivasis and Dalits to safeguard their rights and privileges. At the same time, the Church is not reluctant to stage 'dharnas' and protest rallies to attain her minority privileges and to protect her institutions and other programmes. Though the ecclesiastical bodies are capable of upholding the conditions of the poor sections of society, they take less interest in it. In this situation, the Church as a sign of New Humanity has a significant role to play in politics. Does the Church become the sign of New Humanity in Christ in protecting the interests of ordinary people instead of communal interests?

According to M.M. Thomas, the "Church is not just to look after their communal interests but also perhaps primarily the interests of all men, women and children in the country as human beings."[19] He criticised the attitude of the Church to

---

[19] M. M. Thomas, "The Churches and the Future of Indian Democracy" *NCCR Vol. XCVII / No.6-7* (June-July, 1977) : 343.

keep away from the victims of Emergency from the above-mentioned line of political thought. Does today's Church look after the interests of common people? When the Church stands for a common cause, the tension between the Church and the State cannot be avoided. This is very clearly stated by M.M. Thomas: "The church has every Christian reason to stand for a path of social development which does not deny men and women the dignity of freedom. So long as the church is true to its mission of confessing Christ's 'New Humanity' in society and state, some tensions between church and society, between church and state are inevitable."[20] But in order to avoid tension, churches express their concern for the poor without disturbing the status quo.

According to M.M. Thomas, the main factor that prevents the Church from organised political struggle for social change is that "there are many who sincerely maintain that the movement of church unity, evangelistic mission and even Christian social service will lose their spiritual integrity, if it is mixed up with politics."[21] This approach of non-political Christianity is highly widespread in the Church. It hinders the vision of the New Humanity concept of the Church for new societies and cultures. Since the modern world promotes the freedom to create new things, new societies and new men, the Church cannot stand as a mute spectator in the political sphere.[22] As a sign of New Humanity in Christ, the Church is not only for the works of individual salvation and charitable works, but also for organised collective action to effect changes in society.

---

[20] *Ibid.,* 43.

[21] M. M. Thomas, *Church and Human Community* (Delhi: ISPCK, 1985), 11.

[22] M. M. Thomas, *New Creation in Christ,* 75.

M.M. Thomas views that an open secular state alone can do justice to human freedom in a situation of religious and ideological pluralism.[23] In this context, the Church, the sign and sacrament of New Humanity, is accountable for following an inclusive approach to create an atmosphere of secular human fellowship to prevent religion from being used as a tool of politics. He argues that the Church should participate in the political process, not for its own advantage but for the benefit of society. He believes that the responsible participation of Christians in the secular political realm requires the discrimination between human (creaturely) and inhuman (idolatrous) activities.[24] Inhuman practices involve corruption, violation of democratic rights, negation of freedom of speech, etc. The Church's political participation should not be limited to elections and other political benefits: It should conscientise the unfortunate illiterate people about their political rights and privileges. M.M. Thomas relates corruptibility of power to injustice. According to him, "the corruptibility of power is the main cause of injustice."[25] He continues to say that "because of the corruptibility of power, the existence of irresponsible centres of power and inequality in the distribution are the chief sources of injustice in the world."[26] In short, the Church's political mission is the eradication of corruption and injustice in the world of politics. Regarding political participation, the Church should be aware of the hidden agenda of political parties in the involvement of the struggles of marginalised groups. The goal of political parties may not be similar to the goal of the Church in those struggles.

---

[23] M. M. Thomas, *Church and Human Community*, 47.

[24] M. M. Thomas, *Some Theological Dialogues*, 71.

[25] M. M. Thomas, *Ideological Quest within Christian Commitment*, 42.

[26] *Ibid.*, 131.

In this context, the Church should direct the political parties to the ideologies that uphold the values of New Humanity.

M.M. Thomas clearly explains the role of the Church in the political process. He views that the "church should differentiate its political approach in relation with its ecclesiastical matters and non-ecclesiastical affairs."[27] The Church is not for any political party; it does not seek any political advantage. But the Church should teach its moral teachings to people and should uphold human dignity, human rights and welfare of all. The Church must always be critical of inhuman laws and must creatively respond to them.[28] In order to carry out the political mission of the Church, to put it in the words of Thomas, "Christian ecumenism can become the foundation for a genuine humanism .... as they become involved in preaching truth to power and exercise not merely the diakonia of charity but also of political justice."[29]

M.M. Thomas understands that "the church's witness in the world of politics requires radical renewal in the spirituality and theology of the church."[30] This renewal in the spirituality serves the people to raise voice against injustice and helps to liberate them from self-righteousness. He views that "this spirituality becomes real to the Christian people as they take seriously their participation in power-political movements for justice and their participation in the Eucharistic communion, i.e., as they move between community involved in ideological-

---

[27] M. M. Thomas, *Bharathathil Christava Sabhayude Samuhika Dharmam* (Thiruvalla: The TLC, 1981), 142.

[28] *Ibid.*

[29] M. M. Thomas, *Towards a Theology of Contemporary Ecumenism,* 174.

[30] M. M. Thomas, *Church and Human Community,* 22.

political action and the community of forgiveness."³¹ So the Church's religious concern is not only for preaching gospel, but also for active participation in politics to combat injustice and violation of human rights.

As a New Humanity in Christ, the Church is for the ultimate humanisation of all mankind.³² Humanisation here means the welfare of all people and the liberation of oppressed groups from their oppressive structures. By political participation, the ultimate goal of the Church is humanisation. It involves struggles for the protection of the poor, using the political influence of the Church to attain the rights of adivasis and dalits, etc. But today's ecclesiastical bodies are not being motivated to raise voice for the rights of underprivileged classes. Though the Church has strong political influence and voice to settle some of the issues of subaltern groups, it keeps silent in society by forgetting the mission of New Humanity. But the fact is that "Christian churches have the history of political struggles against the government to protect the communal interests such as sanctioning of schools, colleges, hospitals, etc."³³ Today's Church has failed in handling the issues of the people who are struggling in the areas of poverty, rehabilitation, political exploitation and marginalisation in all aspects of social life. Since the Church has been called as the sign of New Humanity, the interests of the people who are deprived of their rights should be the priority for the Church in the political struggle.

---

[31] M. M. Thomas, "A Spirituality for Combat" in *Freedom, Love Community* edited by K.M. George (Madras: The CLS, 1985), 36.

[32] M. M. Thomas, *Salvation and Humanization* (Madras: The CLS, 1971), 19.

[33] M. M. Thomas, *Parivarthanathinte Daivasasthram* (Thiruvalla: The TLC, 1982), 134.

A Community against Otherness

M.M. Thomas relates the concept of New Humanity to the context of plurality of religions and explains the role of the Church in line with New Humanity in a multi-religious and ideological atmosphere. According to him, "the churches today face no greater challenge than ... their search for human community and in their effort to redefine the meaning of Christ, the church and the Christian mission ..."[34] In the midst of the diversity of religions, what is new today is that they move from isolated existence to dialogical existence.[35] It means that the attitude of inclusiveness has been created among the religions. It is closely related to the implications of New Humanity, that is, abolition of religious exclusiveness. In relation to this approach, M. M. Thomas highlights the mission of the Church in the pluralistic context in this way,

> The church's witness to Christ consists in entering into partnership with men of other religions and secular faiths in the struggle for a 'secular koinonia,' learning from them at some points and correcting them at others, and at the same time pointing to Jesus Christ as the source and goal and criterion of the New Humanity they seek.[36]

But the Christian-non-Christian partnership should be for humanisation of community life. [37] Does the Church follow this approach in the present time? As a sign of New Humanity in Christ, the present Church very often fails to accommodate people of other faiths for the humanisation of society. What we need today is a deep-rooted dialogical relation among

---

[34] M. M. Thomas, *Risking Christ for Christ's Sake* (Geneva: WCC Publications, 1987), VIII.

[35] *Ibid.*, 1.

[36] M. M. Thomas, *New Creation in Christ*, 48.

[37] *Ibid.*, 43.

religions to root out present social issues like fundamentalism, communalism and religious conflicts and riots.

M.M. Thomas suggests that Christians should be fully engaged in serious dialogue with other religions. Referring to the dialogue with living religions, he says that, "dialogue should be aimed at the development of a common secular anthropology as the basis of common action in politics, economics and society in our religiously pluralistic situation."[38] Thus inter-faith dialogue is integral to people's struggle for a new quality of life. The renewal of humanity in Christ is the goal of the Church's dialogue with other faiths. It is an important characteristic of New Humanity in Christ. So dialogue with ideologies and other religions can be considered as the signs of New Humanity given to all mankind in Christ.[39] S. J. Samartha defines dialogue as "an attempt to understand and express our particularity not just in terms of our own heritage but also in relating to the spiritual heritage of our neighbours."[40] He suggests that Christians must approach dialogue from a theo-centric rather than a Christo-centric basis. The dialogue is for liberation from particular religious bondage to have new relations with our neighbours in the larger community.[41] Since New Humanity envisages the renewal of the whole mankind and ideologies, dialogue with other faiths should be taken as the criteria for the realisation of New Humanity in the multi-religious context. There is no hindrance for dialogue because "Christ is

---

[38] M. M. Thomas, *Church and Human Community*, 31.

[39] M. M. Thomas, *Man and the Universe of Faiths* (Madras: The CLS, 1975), 145.

[40] Harold Coward, *Pluralism in the World Religions* (Oxford: One World Publications, 2000), 52.

[41] *Ibid.*, 51.

abolishing or at least lowering the walls of religious exclusiveness in a common response of all religions to the New Humanity in Christ." [42]

M.M. Thomas maintains that the mission of the Church in the pluralistic context must be related to the common human challenge.[43] Here the mission shows the development of human society. It should not be restricted to any particular community or group. By human challenge, we may mean religious fanaticism and communal riots in the multi religious scenario. In this context, "the common response to the problems of humanization is the most fruitful point of entry for a meeting of faiths.[44] If the Church is the sign of the New Humanity in Christ, "the church's mission in the pluralistic context is to discern that the New Humanity of God's creation in Christ is renewing human life outside the church. So Christians should enter into partnership with people of other religions and of no religion in the struggle for a new society upholding justice and human rights."[45]

Thomas comments that the focus of the Church in relation to other faiths is to redeem the human values of freedom, equality and justice and to uphold the quality of national fraternity.[46] In short, the Church's dialogical relation to other faiths is not only to create a peaceful situation and religious harmony, but also to enhance the human values of justice,

---

[42] M. M. Thomas, *The Gospel of Forgiveness and Koinonia*, 9.

[43] M. M. Thomas, *The Church's Mission and Post Modern Humanism*, (Delhi: ISPCK and Thiruvalla: CSS, 1996), 130.

[44] M. M. Thomas, *Man and the Universe of Faiths*, VI.

[45] T. Jacob Thomas, ed. *M.M. Thomas Reader* (Thiruvalla: CSS, 2002), 12.

[46] M. M. Thomas, *The Church's Mission and Post Modern Humanism*, 29.

freedom, equality, etc. How and to what extent the Church responds to common human challenges in the pluralistic context of our time is noticeable.

According to M. M. Thomas, "New Humanity in Christ transforms other religions and atheistic ideologies and takes new and diverse forms in them.[47] For him, this New Humanity in Christ has ability to renew all religions and ideologies.[48] As a transforming force, the Church should enter into dialogue with other faiths for the sake of the renewal of human community. Is the Church becoming a transforming force today? If the Church is not able to become a channel of transformation in the pluralistic context, it cannot be the sign of New Humanity in Christ. This New Humanity in Christ not only renews the human life inside the Church, but also outside the Church. In the context of multi-faiths, M.M. Thomas observes that the divine commission of the Church is to witness the Gospel that renews all world communities in Christ.[49] So as a source of renewal and new creation, the Church cannot be an exclusive community rather an inclusive community that accommodates all groups of people who believe and follow different religions and ideologies. The Church is the guide of all humanity to New Humanity in Christ. That is why M. M. Thomas said, the "Church's witness to Christ consists in entering into fellowship or partnership with men of other faiths."[50]

---

[47] M. M. Thomas, *Risking Christ for Christ's Sake*, 119.

[48] M. M. Thomas, *Parivarthanathinte Daivasasthram*, 123.

[49] M. M. Thomas, *Yesuchristuvil Oru Puthiya Manushian* [Mal.] (Thiruvalla: CLS, 1983), 48.

[50] M. M. Thomas, *New Creation in Christ*, 48.

M.M. Thomas observes that people of New Humanity in Christ are "already released from the absolute claim of religions and quasi-religions, in so far as they are caught up in the New Humanity of Christ."[51] They even enter into dialogue with other religions within the context of a concern for secular human fellowship outside the Church. Here we see two processes—secularisation and relativisation. What is substantiated here is that "New Humanity in Christ, which is characterized by liberating faith and grace, are present and can be discerned anywhere outside the church. The realities of faith and grace outside the church to which the church must open itself if it is to be the church, the nucleus of New Humanity."[52] So a secular human fellowship, which is centred on Christ for the renewal and transformation of humanity, is envisaged by the religious dimension of New Humanity.

A relevant question regarding secular human fellowship outside the Church is, "How does the church discern and open itself to and become a sign of New Humanity in Christ present outside the church? Thomas answers that it can be done only by the church extending the hand of fellowship to other religions."[53] Though Thomas prefers a form of church outside the Church or unbaptised koinonia through dialogue, how and to what extent it is applicable is to be understood in the context of today's Church, which is called as a closed religious community.

M.M. Thomas understands the religious dialogue in the context of justice. He says that "religious dialogue between Christianity, Hinduism and Secular ideologies has relevance

---

[51] M. M. Thomas, *Man and the Universe of Faiths*, 149.

[52] M. M. Thomas, *Some Theological Dialogues*, 113.

[53] *Ibid.*, 115.

to India's search for a spiritual framework for our political struggles for justice without forgetting that our ultimate destiny is reconciliation and social communion."[54] The New Humanity, which promotes inter-faith relations as a part of humanisation, primarily focuses on justice. Since New Humanity in Christ involves the whole humanity irrespective of caste, religion and class, the main duty of the Church is to transform the world communities based on brotherhood and mutual acceptance. The question is, Does today's Church engage in inter-faith dialogue to put down fundamentalism and other religious issues of the present time? Does the Church sincerely take initiative to become an inclusive community in the light of the New Humanity concept?

Communal violence is a grave threat in the present multi-religious scenario. Religious fundamentalism of Muslims and Hindu fanaticism are the result of communalism. It causes religious disharmony, violence, suffering and loss of human lives. Communalism is a global issue. Communalism has become a growing menace. In the midst of severe religious disharmony caused by communalism, what is the role the Church today as a sign of New Humanity? Is the Church responding to the issue of communalism in the present time? However, very often, the Church is not motivated to embrace New Humanity, which stands for harmony and reconciliation. The Church keeps silence and forgets its duty to spread the message of harmony in the time of brutal killings and violence among communities in the name of religion. The Church, the sign of New Humanity in Christ, cannot evade the responsibility for responding to communalism in order to usher in a harmonious community, because New Humanity is characterised by the message of peace, harmony and reconciliation. Communalism and religious disharmony in

---

[54] M. M. Thomas, *Religion and the Revolt of the Oppressed*, 69.

society can be reduced through inter-faith dialogue. Dialogue can bring peace by reducing and eventually eradicating confrontation. The mission of the Church in a multi-religious society is to witness the message of New Humanity, which fosters religious inclusivism, reconciliation, secular human fellowship, etc.

A Kingdom Community

The Church is the sign and sacrament of New Humanity. So the Church is to be characterised by the qualities of New Humanity in Christ. Does the Church experience the qualities of New Humanity in the present context? In the fuller sense, today's Church is not emerging as New Humanity in Christ.

According to M.M. Thomas, "New Humanity is based on the common acknowledgement of divine forgiveness in Christ and therefore of the need of mutual forgiveness."[55] It implies that as New Humanity in Christ, the Church is the source of divine forgiveness and thereby mutual forgiveness. Instead of being a channel of forgiveness, the Church has become more institutionalised in the modern period. Vested interests, money-oriented values, separatism, self-centeredness, etc., prevent the Church from becoming New Humanity in Christ. For, M.M. Thomas New Humanity is a reality that destroys all divisions.[56] It means New Humanity in Christ promotes no division based on caste, colour, status, sex, etc., and breaks all barriers or walls of partition. It echoes the Pauline concept of oneness in Christ, which upholds the virtue of reconciliation. But it is sad to note that the Church in the present context is gripped by all types of divisions.

---

[55] M. M. Thomas, *New Creation in Christ*, 5.

[56] M. M. Thomas, *Christava Samuhya Dharmam* [Mal.] (Thiruvalla: The TLC, 1972), 34.

By New Humanity, the Church is meant to witness fellowship in Christ. Through the fellowship in Christ a new community of God's people and a new human society are emerging. M.M. Thomas observes that, "Fellowship in Christ is realized as a sacramental reality in the religious life of the church around the Bible and the Lord's table." [57] In the sacramental fellowship of the Church, the emergence of a new reality, a new humanity, can be seen. Since the Church is the community of sacramental fellowship, it is the duty of the Church to witness a new society that is based on the fellowship in Christ and social fellowship based on Christ, the source of new creation.[58] The new society, which is created out of sacramental fellowship, is realised in the context of fellowship within the community rather than the ritualistic aspect. The cross of Jesus is the basis of the fellowship that transcends all divisions. That is why M.M. Thomas viewed, "Cross of Jesus as the only ultimate criterion for truth and the place where true fellowship transcending our divisions can be found and renewed."[59] The fellowship in Christ aims at identification with the poor people in the congregation without any discrimination. It means, mission of the Church is bringing people into the fellowship in Christ. So the "church is essentially people oriented in Christ to God and the world; and to God's purpose for the world."[60] The purpose of the Church is to bring transformation within the Church and in various sectors of human community.

M.M. Thomas understands New Humanity in Christ in the context of Christian ecumenism. It is the ground and pillar

---

[57] M. M. Thomas, *New Creation in Christ*, 43.

[58] *Ibid.*, 46.

[59] *Ibid.*, 58.

[60] M. M. Thomas, *Church and Human Community*, 39.

of New Humanism. Thus, he holds that "Christian ecumenism has truth and meaning only as it becomes the ground and pillar of a New Humanism."[61] So, an ecumenical atmosphere among different denominations is necessary for the realisation of New Humanity in Christ. This ecumenical approach "should involve the churches more effectively in mission and service to the larger community."[62] "It is not merely the matter of inter-ecclesiastical relations but is closely related to church's task in and for the world."[63] So, the Church, the sign of New Humanity, is to be united beyond all differences. Then only the Church can work for the transformation of ecclesiastical arena and world communities. This ecumenical endeavour has another dimension, i.e., social justice. M.M.Thomas observes that "Ecumenism in India will remain frustrated until questions of social justice are regarded as integral to evangelism and church dogmatics."[64] Social mission, which is an integral part of New Humanity, is emphasised in relation to ecumenism.

New Humanity in Christ is characterised by forgiveness, reconciliation, genuine fellowship and Christian ecumenism. However, an important issue today is whether the Church is emerging as a sign of New Humanity in the present ecclesiastical scenario. Very often, the Church fails to emerge as a realm of New Humanity because of internal problems.

---

[61] M. M. Thomas, *Towards a Theology of Contemporary Ecumenism*, 164.

[62] M. M. Thomas, "Promotion of World Development Services and the Problem of Relationships" *Religion and Society*, Vol. 19/ No. 3 (1972): 45.

[63] M. M. Thomas, "Spirituality for Combat", *NCCR*, Vol. XCVI / No.1 (Jan.-1976):38.

[64] M.M. Thomas, *Religion and the Revolt of the Oppressed*, 16.

The conflict between the rich and the poor, communal feelings, individualism, disunity among believers, struggle for power, etc., prevent the Church from upholding the values of New Humanity in Christ. Since the Church is more than a religious reality, it cannot be silent to social issues. If the Church is not able to respond to human issues because of internal problems, it will destroy the very idea of the Church as a fellowship in Christ. The Church is called to witness the new life in Christ and to become sign and sacrament of New Humanity.

A Community of Cosmic Renewal

M.M. Thomas relates the concept of New Humanity with nature. He says, "God constantly renews the New Humanity and thus makes all things new. He gives a new human nature, a new humanity and a new cosmos."[65] Here the renewal of the cosmos is described as a part of the creation of New Humanity in Christ. Since renewal of all things is the basis of New Humanity, M.M. Thomas observes that, "Christ brings renewal, not only to the inner being of man, not only to human relations in society, but also to the whole cosmos – 'all' things in heaven and earth."[66]

The Gospel of Christ has a message of renewal of all things. This renewal is not limited to human beings alone because the wholeness of man includes man's relation to the material world and sub-human creation. The purpose of the renewal of all things in Christ is to prevent the world from becoming perverse and dehumanising.[67] In the context of the exploitation of nature, M.M. Thomas mentions the mission of the Church as a sign of New Humanity that upholds newness in life in

---

[65] M. M. Thomas, *New Creation in Christ*, 7.
[66] Ibid., 6.
[67] Ibid., 7.

this way: "if Christ's mission is to renew the world for God, it is also the mission of the church of Christ. The church is not just a religious institution but people acknowledging God's renewal of all things in Christ."[68] Here the duty of the Church is to protect nature from all kinds of exploitation and thereby renew the whole cosmos. He continues to say that "the church must be prepared to stand by the people when they struggle for an economy that gives priority to eco-justice and social-justice rather than economic growth through transnational high technology.[69] In the context of globalisation and consumerism, which exploit nature for the benefits of multinational companies, the mission of the Church as a sign of New Humanity is to stand for the renewal of the cosmos.

According to M.M. Thomas, "the community of those who believe in Christ is to be a witness to the renewal of all things in Christ."[70] Christ is the true man and source of newness and renewal of human nature and through it of all things. The liberation of Jesus to humankind involves the affirmation of his Lordship over all natural and cosmic powers.[71] So liberation in Christ given to mankind affirms the fact that the mission of Christ is the liberation of the cosmos from all kinds of degradation and exploitation. Thus the mission of the Church, the sign of New Humanity, is nothing more than that. The Lordship of Christ is clearly depicted in Colossians

---

[68] M. M. Thomas, *The Gospel of Forgiveness and Koinonia*, 59.

[69] M. M. Thomas, *The Church's Mission and Post-Modern Humanism*, 127.

[70] M. M. Thomas, "The Secular Ideologies of India and the Secular Meaning of Christ" in *Readings in Indian Christian Theology, Vol. 1*, edited by R. S. Sugirtharajah and Cecil Hargreaves (Delhi : ISPCK, 1993), 94.

[71] *Ibid.*, 97.

1:16-20: "In Him all things were created, in heaven and on earth, visible and invisible—whether thrones or dominions or principalities or authorities—all things were created through him and for him. He is before all things, and in him all things hold together—in him all the fullness of God was pleased to dwell and through him to reconcile to himself all things; whether on earth or in heaven, making peace by the blood of his cross."[72]

M.M. Thomas connects Romans chapter 8 with New Humanity. Romans 8 shows that the whole creation is groaning in the hope for the day of renewal. He comments that "the redeeming Gospel of new creation in Christ has a total scope, including renewal of the human nature, a new humanity and a new cosmos." [73] In the context of ecological concerns and issues, he argues for a close relation between eco-justice and social justice. According to him, "Eco-justice and social justice are both extremely important for the livelihood of dalits, tribals, women, fisher folk, etc. Eco-justice divorced from social justice makes the struggle for environmental issues just another middle-class concern." [74]

What is the response of the Church, the sign of New Humanity, which is for the renewal of the whole cosmos in the midst of ecological issues? The Church in the present time fails to respond properly to ecological problems. Today, nature has been considered as a mere object. Human beings feel free to change nature for their own purpose and interest. In the context of ecological issues such as sand mining, pollution from multinational companies and the development that destroys flora and fauna, the Church as a New Humanity in

---

[72] *Ibid.*, 99.

[73] Hielke T. Wolters, *Theology of Prophetic Participation*, 99.

[74] *Ibid.*, 251.

A Community of Audacious Mission

M. M. Thomas understands the struggles of people for the dignity of selfhood, their right to participate in power and for their struggle of bread and life in the context of New Humanity in Christ.[75] This New Humanity offers a fuller and richer human life[76] and it is the role of the Church to express its solidarity with those people who search for richer and fuller human life, especially Dalits and Tribals. He relates the salvation and its realisation to the struggles of poor people. So, M.M.Thomas observed that "there can be no understanding or realization of God and salvation or the life and mission of the church except in full solidarity with the world, with men in their struggles and achievements and hopes and frustrations."[77] Instead of supporting the struggles of oppressed groups, the Church follows the idea of non-political Christianity and continues the works of individual salvation and other charitable works. The Church is afraid of participating in organising the oppressed Dalits of this land or leading them in organised struggles against the oppressive caste, class, power structures existing in this land to secure social justice.[78] As a sign of New Humanity in Christ, the Church has failed to express its solidarity with the struggles of Dalits to secure social justice.

In the context of the awakening of new consciousness among the oppressed Dalit groups, that is, awareness of self-

---

[75] M. M. Thomas, *Towards a Theology of Contemporary Ecumenism*, 216.

[76] M. M. Thomas, *Salvation and Humanization*, 4.

[77] M. M. Thomas, *New Creation in Christ*, 63.

[78] M. M. Thomas, *Church and Human Community*, 22.

love, self-affirmation and pride, M.M. Thomas identifies that "Christians need to hear the cry for a revolutionary understanding of the oppressed because all quest for richer and fuller human life is the work of Christ." [79] But today's Church gives less importance to the struggles of Dalits who search for social justice and fuller human life. At the same time, the Church is not backward in participating in the struggles of established institutions run by different ecclesiastical bodies. As M.M. Thomas noted in Salvation and Humanization, "Christian community is not one self-regarding minority community competing with other religious communities. On the other hand, it is the creative minority which is the servant of all communities." [80] It means that the Church is not concerned only with the interests of its own people; as a sign of New Humanity in Christ, it represents all people in the world. It is for the protection of weaker sections of society and for the freedom of all people. Since New Humanity focuses on renewal and transformation of the whole society, it is the mission of the Church to intentionally engage with the issues of Dalit people.

In the context of Dalit struggles for social justice, equality, fuller human life, as a sign of New Humanity in Christ, the mission of the Church is to "create a new spirituality that refuses to bow down to the dictatorial powers that dehumanize people and to create new forms of community of people relevant to the present time."[81] What we need today

---

[79] V. Devasahayam, "Search for the Last, the Least and the Lost – Dr. M. M. Thomas' understanding of the Humans, God and the New Humanity" in *Christian Witness in Society* edited by K. C. Abraham (Bangalore: BTE-SSC, 1998), 113.

[80] T. Jacob Thomas, ed. *M. M. Thomas Reader...*, 12.

[81] *Ibid.*, 134.

for the upliftment of marginalised groups is the rediscovery of the Christ of the poor and the oppressed for the solidarity and identification of the Church with those who are struggling for liberation.[82] Struggles of Dalits against oppressive structures should be seen in the context of New Humanity in Christ. Whether the Church does respond to the Dalit issues of human rights violation, marginalisation in the areas of social and religious life, is a crucial question about the mission of the Church.

Tribals are the most exploited or ill-treated people. They are economically poor and politically powerless. They face serious problems because of ecological crisis and exploitation. The most important issue the tribals face today is deforestation and displacement. Because of the developmental projects of multinational companies, they are forced to leave their homeland, i.e., forests. They also struggle for social status, their autonomy and their right for land. They struggle a lot to survive in the midst of these issues. Though they have their own land and resources, they are prevented from taking the land officially by the government. In order to establish their rights over the forest land, they have attempted many struggles in the past days. Today's tribal society is in the path of awakening and is conscious of their rights. M.M. Thomas says, "The awakening of all primal people today is grounded on their new self-understanding that they are active subjects of history instead of its passive objects." [83]

As a sign of New Humanity in Christ, the Church cannot ignore the struggles of tribal society because New Humanity stands for the humanisation of the marginalised. In the context of tribal struggles:

---

[82] *Ibid.*, 140.

[83] M. M. Thomas, *Man and the Universe of Faiths*, 58.

> The mission of the church is to be present within the creative liberation movements of our time ... and so participate in them as to be able to communicate the genuine gospel of liberation—from vicious circle of sin and alienation, law and self-righteousness and frustration and death—into the realm of Christ's new humanity where there is forgiveness and reconciliation, grace and justification, and renewal and eternal life.[84]

So the duty of the Church is to participate and encourage the struggles of forest people for new life and renewal in the light of gospel. But very often, the Church fails to do the same. The task of the Church should be to discern Christ, who is present in the human quest, in the life of tribal people. Here M.M. Thomas observes that "the divine commission of church is to witness the Gospel which renews all world communities in Christ." [85] Renewal in Christ points to the liberation of all people groups from destructive forces.

The concept of New Humanity in Christ explains that the Church is called to involve and respond to the struggles of human life. Humanisation is the basis of New Humanity. Since the Church is a sign and sacrament of New Humanity, the mission of the Church is for an egalitarian society that upholds the values of justice, human dignity, etc. But how far the Church responds to issues of contemporary society in the light of New Humanity is a crucial question today. The concept of New Humanity does not promote an approach of non-political Christianity because the Church is for the transformation of society, even through political struggles. The focus of the Church in relation to other faiths is to narrow down the walls of religious exclusiveness through dialogue in order to realise religious harmony and development of human society.

---

[84] T. Jacob Thomas, ed. *M. M. Thomas Reader...*, 27.

[85] M. M. Thomas, *Yesuchristuvil Oru Puthiya Manushyan* [Mal.], 48.

M. M. Thomas understands that the Church is to witness the values of New Humanity not only in society, but also within the ecclesiastical sphere. New humanity has another dimension, that is, ecological. Social justice and eco-justice are integrally related to each other. Since New Humanity in Christ stands for humanisation and renewal, the Church should identify and participate in the struggles of marginalised and oppressed Dalits and Tribals. To what extent the Church is accountable for its mission of New Humanity has to be discussed at respective social locations.

Chapter 5
The Theology of Paulose Mar Paulose

Paulose Mar Paulose, a radical Indian theologian of the twentieth century, attempted to provide a new meaning to the witness of the Church through his participation in the socio-political issues of his time. His theological method began with a re-reading of the Scripture. He developed his theology from the perspective of universal humanhood. As a theologian who affirmed secularism, he interpreted the Gospel in conversation with secular ideologies and non-Christian faith traditions of India. The major focuses of Mar Paulose were issues such as poverty, human rights violation, fundamentalism, rights of the under privileged people and the like. In this chapter, his theological method and theology are presented. A biographical sketch and major influences on his theology are also included.

Paulose Mar Paulose: The Man and his Context
Paulose Mar Paulose was born on 14th September 1941 at Chirayathu in Trissur district, Kerala, as the youngest son of

Konikkara Antony and Kochu Mariam. He did his studies at Chaldean Syrian High School, Trissur, and St. Thomas College, Trissur. He received his theological education from Serampore College, Serampore. He was ordained as deacon of the Chaldean Syrian Church in 1958 and as priest in 1965. In 1968, he was consecrated as Bishop, Chaldean Syrian Church. He went to the USA for his graduate studies. He took his Th.M. from Princeton Theological Seminary. Mar Paulose earned his Ph.D. from Graduate Theological Union, Berkeley, California, and the title of his dissertation was "A Bonhoefferian Corrective of Karl Marx's Critique of Religion."[1] While he was in Berkeley, he participated in the protests against the Vietnam War. He also witnessed the student protests at Tiananmen Square in China in 1989.[2]

After his studies abroad, Mar Paulose came back to India, when the country was under Internal Emergency. Since he was deeply concerned about the violation of civil liberties and fundamental rights of the people, he joined M. M. Thomas and others who opposed the Emergency and actively participated in programmes for helping the victims of the Emergency. He was Chairman, Student Christian Movement, Kerala Region, for two terms. He also served as President, Indian Chapter of Christian Peace Conference and as Chairman, World Student Christian Federation. He also served as Secretary of the Episcopal Synod of his church. He died on 24th March 1998.

According to Mar Meletius, "Paulose Mar Paulose was less concerned about the dogmas and doctrines of the church that often only helped to torture Jesus by dividing his community

---

[1] Paulose Mar Paulose, *Encounter in Humanization* (Thiruvalla: CSS, 2000), 8-9.

[2] Paulose Mar Paulose, *Swathanthryamanu Daivam* (Malayalam) (Ariyannur: *Patabhedam*, 1996), 2.

than about the plights of millions of people in this very world which Jesus came to liberate."³ Mar Paulose was against the institutionalisation of justice in the name of religion and God. He believed in the liberation of people from their social, political, economic and religious oppression. For him, human beings are essentially political beings and so they should actively participate in the political process. Such political involvements help to evolve a free and just society. He also believed that liberation is a common concern of humanity, irrespective of religion and ideology. Those who believe in God cannot be kept away from joining hands with those who struggle for justice and liberation.⁴

Paulose Mar Paulose was a staunch advocate of human rights. His approach was prophetic, and he participated in the struggles for justice: "As a prophet he spoke with clarity, vigor and boldness. He was listened to with great interest perhaps more outside than inside the Church. He was re-reading the Bible in solidarity with the marginalized in their struggles for justice and peace."⁵ He was ready to be arrested during the emergency. He faced severe opposition from his Church and from other conservative Christians due to his co-operation with the leftist movements. He had involved himself as a mediator to settle many strikes in Kerala, and his mediations to solve the strike of the head-load workers in Trissur and the student strike at the Kerala University are noteworthy.⁶

---

³ *Ibid.*, 7.

⁴ *Ibid.*

⁵ Paulose Mar Paulose, *Spirituality for Struggle* (Tiruvalla: CSS, 1999), Back cover page.

⁶ Paulose Mar Paulose, *Nisabdharayirikkan Ningalkkenthadhikaram* (Malayalam) (Noorannad: Fabian Books, 1998), 124.

The significance of the life, witness and theology of Paulose Mar Paulose is well stated in the testimonies of several cultural and political activists. For E.M.S. Nambudhiripad, the first Chief Minister of Kerala and a prominent communist idealogue, "the vision of Paulose Mar Paulose is genuinely Christian. It's not communism; rather, a vision that combines true Christianity and Communism in order to serve people."[7] Sukumar Azhikode, a famous writer and cultural activist, testified Mar Paulose as a fearless Bishop who tried to realise the essence of Jesus' religion that upholds human welfare and equality.[8] According to P. Govinda Pillai, a communist idealogue, "his doctoral dissertation, apart from its deep erudition, strongly puts forth his passion for the liberation of the exploited and the marginalized. In spite of being a priest, he was so daring to risk his life."[9] According to Ninan Koshy, a close associate of Mar Paulose, "Paulose Mar Paulose developed a progressive social vision based on Christian faith. He always sided with the struggles of the oppressed people for their rights and liberation. His spirituality was one that strengthens and encourages the struggles of the people."[10] In short, the life and witness of Paulose Mar Paulose was a struggle to bring about radical changes in the approach of institutionalised churches in order to address the issues of the people to strive for a just world.

Major Influences on the Theology of Paulose Mar Paulose

Paulose Mar Paulose was a secular theologian with a deep commitment to the world around him. His theological assumptions were always related to contemporary socio-

---

[7] *Ibid.*, 118.

[8] *Ibid.*, 120-121.

[9] *Ibid.*, 123.

[10] *Ibid.*, 134.

political and religious issues. His faith in God compelled him to get involved in the life of society for the affirmation of the rights of all people. For him, Christian faith was an invitation to engage in social transformation. In his theological journey, Paulose Mar Paulose was influenced not only by theologians, but also by various secular peoples' movements. Some of the major influences are briefly described in this section.

The Berkely Experience

Mar Paulose was a graduate student at Berkely during the time of the Vietnam War. Berkeley was known for its student protests against the American foreign policy on the Vietnam War. The student protests were a turning point in his theological thinking. As Mar Paulose rightly puts it, "the students' protests in Berkely sowed the seeds of protest and resistance in my life against the forces of injustice."[11] Life at Berkely taught him the spirit and radical meaning of Christian obedience. He was convinced that on certain occasions, Christian obedience needs to be demonstrated through resistance.[12]

Marxian Humanism

During his time at Berkeley, Mar Paulose was influenced by the humanism of Karl Marx.[13] Marxian humanism affirms the value and dignity of human beings. The decisive productive force of history is the human person at work in all spheres of creative activity in production, discovery, and invention, artistic creation and political and moral decisions. Human beings make their own history. They are socially active natural beings and not just natural beings. Humans are what they are

---

[11] Paulose Mar Paulose, *Swathanthryamanu Daivam*, 7.

[12] *Ibid.*

[13] Paulose Mar Paulose, *Encounter in Humanization*, 8.

concretely in society and in nature. But they are deprived of liberty, enslaved and made an instrument. Thus they are alienated. A re-integration of humans with nature can return them to their true nature. Marx does not accept the Christian understanding of human beings, which begins and ends with God—the source of all human actuality and potentiality.[14] Regarding the description of Marxian Humanism in the dissertation of Paulose Mar Paulose, E. M. S Nambudhiripad indirectly criticises him that Paulose Mar Paulose does not see the essence of Marxian Humanism, i.e., the creation of a classless society.[15] According to Ninan Koshy, "Marx influenced Paulose Mar Paulose in terms of Marxian idea of commitment to human being and struggle."[16] It can be argued that Mar Paulose must have involved in and supported the people's movements of his time because of the profound influence of Marxian Humanism on his thinking. Marxian affirmation of human autonomy and dignity would have persuaded Mar Paulose to raise his voice against the dehumanising tendencies in society that alienate humans from each other.

The Religionless Christianity of Dietrich Bonhoeffer

Dietrich Bonhoeffer was a major influence on the development of the theology of Paulose Mar Paulose. The influence of the concept of Bonhoefferian Religionless Christianity is very important.[17] The religionless Christianity of Bonhoeffer affirms that human life is meaningful only if it is dutiful to God, and

---

[14] *Ibid.*, 96-101

[15] Paulose Mar Paulose, *Nisabdharayirikkan Ningalkkenthadhikaram*, 116. They are Marxists who had problems with Mar Paulose's understanding of humanism.

[16] Interview with Prof. Ninan Koshy, Trivandrum, 24th April 2007.

[17] Paulose Mar Paulose, *Swathanthryamanu Daivam*, 7.

faith is the negation of religion. Bonhoeffer provides three guidelines for the life of a 'religionless Christian.' They are 'Holy Worldliness,' 'Theology of Responsibility' and 'Secret Discipline.' Holy worldliness means a complete dedication to life, a commitment to one's potential and to the needs of the world. Theology of responsibility refers to a pragmatic human response to the demand of God and the need of the neighbours. Secret Discipline means maintaining the relationship with the Divine and being sensitive to human realities. It directly points to the disciplined Christian life in terms of secular life. The substance of Religionless Christianity is readiness to expand the scope of faith beyond the dogmas and creeds in practical sense.[18] The influence of Religionless Christianity is evident in his attempts for secular and religious interpretation of the Scripture and his engagement in the struggles of society. It is clear when he says, "the criterion for understandability on theological language should not be how well it is understood by the believer but by the non-believer."[19] He always tried to convey his theological convictions understandable to all sections of people irrespective of religion and ideology. He did not regard dogmas and doctrines more important than faith. The statement of Paulose Mar Paulose, "my faith compels me to work both within myself and within the community towards the affirmation of life to all people spiritually, politically, economically and socially"[20] echoes the spirit of Religionless Christianity.

---

[18] Paulose Mar Paulose, *Encounter in Humanization*, 167-175.

[19] Paulose Mar Paulose, "Indian Christian Theology, the Church and the People," *Religion and Society*, Vol.XXX / No 384(September-December, 1983): 89.

[20] Paulose Mar Paulose, *Spirituality for Struggle*, 13.

Political Emergency in India

After his studies at Berkeley, Mar Paulose returned to India, when India was under internal Emergency.[21] The internal Emergency was the outcome of the political developments after the split in the Indian National Congress and the 1971 parliamentary elections. The Government during that time did not respect the spirit of the Constitutional provisions for emergency. Freedom was literally curbed in all aspects of life. The new laws silenced political opponents and censorship was imposed on print and electronic media. Civil rights were negated, and hundreds of poor people were evicted from the slums as part of the beautification of the cities. It is also to be noted that Indian churches were either neutral or in favour of the Emergency except some dissenting voices from a few church leaders and theologians.[22] But the resistance of people against the political Emergency influenced and shaped his thinking.[23] He questioned the negation of civil liberties of people and got involved in the activities for helping the victims.

M. M. Thomas

M.M.Thomas was a real prophet during the Emergency, and Mar Paulose saw the real form of protest and resistance against the Emergency in him. The Emergency gave him another

---

[21] According to the Indian Constitution, Internal Emergency can be declared if there is any internal or external threat to the security of the Nation.

[22] M. M. Thomas, *Response to Tyranny* (New Delhi: Forum for Christian Concern People's Struggle, 1979) & "Christians and the Emergency: Some Documents," *Religion and Society* Vol. XXIV/ No. 2&3 (June-September, 1977).

[23] Paulose Mar Paulose, *Swathanthryamanu Daivam*, 175.

picture of M.M. Thomas. Mar Paulose always acknowledged how he was influenced by the life and thinking of M.M. Thomas. His contact with Thomas helped him to sharpen his understanding of Christian political witness.[24] According to E.M.S. Nambudhiripad, Paulose Mar Paulose completed his theological education through his activities with M.M. Thomas.[25] According to Ninan Koshy, the social commitment of Mar Paulose was the result of the strong impact of Thomas. M.M. Thomas influenced him greatly in reformulating the expression of his faith commitment through participating in the struggles of his time.[26] This profound and direct influence of Thomas must have led Mar Paulose to read the Scripture in relation to the political commitment of Christians towards the socio-political realities of the nation. The involvement of Mar Paulose in the activities of social action groups to combat against social evils and human rights violations could be the outcome of Thomas' influence.

E. M. S. Nambudhiripad

E.M.S. Nambudhiripad (hereafter E.M.S.) has contributed deeply to the theological thinking of Mar Paulose. In fact, he considered E. M. S as his Guru.[27] Pavanan observed that even before his sojourn in the USA for his doctoral programme, Mar Paulose was interested in the writings of E.M.S.[28] According to P. Govinda Pillai, "Mar Paulose had high respect for and interest in E.M.S. It was both ideological and

---

[24] *Ibid.*, 7-8.

[25] Paulose Mar Paulose, *Nisabdharayirikkan Ningalkkenthadhikaram*, 118.

[26] Interview with Prof. Ninan Koshy, Trivandrum, 24th April, 2007.

[27] Paulose Mar Paulose, *Nisabdharayirikkan Ningalkkenthadhikaram*, 133.

[28] *Ibid.*, 131.

emotional."[29] Once, E.M.S. mentioned that instead of expressing their opinions on all matters under the sun, it would have been better if the bishops and priests practiced the way of the Cross in their life. Paulose Mar Paulose responded positively to this statement. For him, the exhortation of E.M.S. was a call to stand along with the voiceless and the powerless and to participate in their struggles.[30] It shows Mar Paulose's intellectual indebtedness to E.M.S. The abovementioned influences on Mar Paulose gave him an intellectual and ideological orientation to develop his theology committed to the life realities of people. He brought 'theology' outside the Church and proclaimed 'Freedom is God.' His boldness to theologise in the context of the struggles of people was the consequence of his engagement with progressive theologians and idealogues and the experiences of people who fought for freedom.

Theological Method of Paulose Mar Paulose

The Indian context that challenged Mar Paulose to develop his theological reflection played a key role in his method of theologising. The emergency questioned the basic civil and human rights of the people and human freedom in all walks of life. Religious fundamentalism and communalism disturbed the pluralistic fabric of society. Economic policies were pushing people into poverty. Patriarchal domination kept women away from the mainstream of society. Dalits and other oppressed communities were under the bondage of the caste system. The churches of his time concentrated on communal politics based on minority consciousness. In such a context, Mar Paulose made an attempt to re-read the text contextually. For that, he started from the context to the text. He challenged theology

---

[29] *Ibid.,* 123.
[30] *Ibid.,* 125.

to compare the biblical experiences with contemporary life experiences and to discern what God wants us to do in the here and now. "We should read the Bible not as a book of law, not as a code of ethics or lack of awareness of modern world. Rather we should read the Bible to get a picture of the Man-Jesus."[31] Mar Paulose further argued that "the Word of God can be relevant only as it assumes new and bold forms in relation to the actual historical situation and the particular needs of the people in their own time."[32] So Gospel should be retold repeatedly in the light of the experiences of people in particular historical situation.

Along with the particular context, M. M. Thomas inspired Mar Paulose to place human issues in his method of theologising. The criticisms and the ideological stimulus of E.M.S. motivated him to read the way of the Cross in relation to the struggles of the people. In his theological attempt, the Bonhoefferian idea of Religionless Christianity influenced Mar Paulose to re-emphasise more on the faith that risks for others than the Church dogmas that de-emphasise the human problems of society. Secular theories such as Marxism, Secularism and Democracy, taught him the meaning and the importance of human rights and values in doing theology. These inputs led Mar Paulose to have a theological method, i.e., "interpreting the world in the light of the Bible."[33] Within this framework, Mar Paulose responded to the social issues through preaching, lectures and writings and personal intervention.[34]

---

[31] Paulose Mar Paulose, *Spirituality for Struggle*, 20.

[32] Ibid., 36.

[33] Paulose Mar Paulose, *Swathanthr yamanu Daivam*, 173

[34] Ibid.,8.

Being an 'un'systematic theologian who never bothered to develop his own theological reflection into a systematic treatise, Mar Paulose always confessed that he would not do theology according to a particular method. His theological reflection emerged when he was emotionally disturbed by visions and dreams or when he was happy after a game of tennis or when he was criticised by his Church members or when he was upset by the unjust practices in society.[35] Even though he never claimed a particular methodology, he always kept five principles while articulating his theological reflections. Firstly, *timeliness*. The task of theology is to make the Word of God relevant to contemporary people. So, timeliness is an essential aspect of doing theology. In India, it means considering the hopes and aspirations of people and their struggles for liberation.[36] Secondly, *substance*. Substance means, we must seriously consider not only the Christian texts, but also the texts of non-Christian traditions, and even the texts that stand in opposition to God, for our theological reflections. He also believed that creative sources such as novel, cinema, art and literature could also become the means by which God speaks to us.[37] Thirdly, *understandability*. Here, Mar Paulose gives emphasis to a secular interpretation of the Bible. The understandability of our theological language is not based on how it is understood by the believer but by the non-believer. In order to understand our theology by all the people, it should be related to the world realities.[38] Fourthly, theology must take into consideration *the larger world outside the Church* in the context of the emergence of the new

---

[35] *Ibid.*,26.

[36] Paulose Mar Paulose, "*Indian Christian Theology....,*" 89.

[37] Paulose Mar Paulose, *Swathanthryamanu Daivam*, 29.

[38] Paulose Mar Paulose, "*Indian Christian Theology....,*" 89.

community. Fifthly, theological endeavour in the present context should be preceded by *an act of negation* or protest or judgment upon the status quo.[39] By negating a negative thing, we affirm the possibility of a new reality, which lies beyond us.[40] It is also to be noted that the theological reflections of Mar Paulose are not within the framework of his Church traditions. At the same time, he does not criticise Church beliefs and practices. But he tried to give a new understanding to the customs of the Church in relation to contemporary social challenges.[41] In his theologising, Mar Paulose interprets world realities, i.e., human struggles, apprehensions, hopes and aspirations in the light of Scripture and divine justice. Therefore, he can be called as theologian of liberation. He placed contextual human issues in his theological engagement.

Theology of Paulose Mar Paulose

The Theology of Paulose Mar Paulose is a conversation between social realities and the Gospel. His theological reflections emerged out of his intentional engagement with human struggles and ideologies. In his theology, Mar Paulose responded to various socio-political and religious issues with an intention to bring about creative transformation. In his

---

[39] It comes from Marx's concept of 'Negation of negation'. According to Marx, the capitalist mode of appropriation produces capitalist private property. This is the first negation of individual private property. But the capitalist production begets, with the inexorability of a law of Nature, its negation. It is the negation of negation (Karl Marx, *Capital* Vol.1, p.715) Here Mar Paulose gives a Christian appropriation of the concept of Negation of negation

[40] Paulose Mar Paulose, "*Indian Christian Theology...*," 90.

[41] Paulose Mar Paulose, *Vithakyappetta Vithukal* (Malayalam) Collection by K. J Thomas (Thrissur: Paulose Mar Paulose Foundation, 2005), 23-30.

biblical hermeneutics, he re-reads the Bible from the perspective of the experiences of the people in order to interpret the world in the light of the Scripture. His theological assumptions were informed not only by the Bible, but also by non-Christian religious traditions and ideologies. In this section, an attempt has been made to give a brief description of the theology of Paulose Mar Paulose.

Doctrine of God

Mar Paulose understood "Freedom as God."[42] According to him, the liberator God whom we see in the Bible can be understood only through love, justice and freedom. He questioned the tendency to project a God who was located in the secret realms of human knowledge.[43] God is committed to the renewal of the world, and it is our responsibility to participate in the Divine project. "God renews this world. His renewal happens in the socio-political-cultural realms of human society. God exhorts humans to take the responsibility along with him to renew this world."[44] God is renewing everything in the world–that is God's promise. God encourages human participation in the process of renewal. Here Christian hope is activated by divine promise and exhortation.[45] Mar Paulose also identified the presence of God in the struggles and the transforming activities of the human community.

> As God spoke in the life of biblical writers and people of old time, God speaks in the struggle of women world over, demanding fullest right of participation in the life of society, in the struggles of poor for justice, in the effort of peace-

---

[42] Paulose Mar Paulose, *Swathanthryamanu Daivam*, 169.

[43] Ibid., 170.

[44] Paulose Mar Paulose *Nisabdharayirikkan Ningalkkenthadhikaram*, 109.

[45] Ibid., 110.

loving people to protest all and every war; in the range of modern society to be free from institutions that lost their meaning, to be free from traditions that lost their roots, to be free from laws that only make it harder to love. God reveals himself in all the joyful and tragic events of everyday life; and we read about it in newspapers.[46]

His understanding of God is a radical shift from God as a transcendent being to an imminent being, who engages with human beings and inspires them to participate in the Divine project of renewal in our midst.

Doctrine of Christ

According to Mar Paulose, "Jesus was a revolutionary who undermined the prevailing political and social stability of his time."[47] He also depicted Christ as the universal being and the Lord of all. Jesus is not only the Lord of the Church, but also of the entire world. The uniqueness of Jesus is his universality.[48] "Since God is giving leadership to all revolutions for the development and prosperity of humanity, Jesus is not only the Lord of the Church, but also of political parties and trade unions and all the movements that work for the transformation of human society."[49] According to Mar Paulose, salvation in Jesus Christ means salvation through the way of Jesus. The way of Jesus is the way of the cross. It is the way of confrontation, suffering and death. Mar Paulose did not want to see Jesus apart from the created world. Jesus is the living truth in us. Christ does not have any significance as a separate entity detached from the human community. Christ

---

[46] Paulose Mar Paulose, *Spirituality for Struggle*, 17.

[47] Ibid., 40.

[48] Paulose Mar Paulose, *Church's Mission* (Bombay: BUILD, n.d.), 17.

[49] Paulose Mar Paulose, *Swathanthryamanu Daivam*, 92.

is beyond myths and traditions.[50] Here he describes Christ as the universal being whose presence can be sensed in all progressive movements and revolutions of people for radical societal transformation. So, Christ-presence can be distinguished by freedom and transformation. Mar Paulose challenged the traditional assumptions of salvation and tried to interpret it in relation to human struggles. He attempted to place Christ along with the existential question of the time.

Christian Obedience

Mar Paulose reinterpreted Christian obedience as resistance. The Gospel reminds us that there are times when resistance is a form of Christian obedience. Under certain circumstances, to be obedient can mean to resist. In the dominant understanding, obedience is passive silence. For him, this was not the right attitude. Resistance is a legitimate part of Christian life and ethics.[51] Here resistance becomes responsibility. It is not a rebellion against anyone, but speaking out. Sometimes, it may hurt both the ruler and the ruled. But resistance is not directed against them. Its focus is a possible creative transformation.[52] In relation to Christian obedience, Mar Paulose suggested that "the Gospel of resistance should be proclaimed to men and women not in isolation but in solidarity. For the Church to proclaim the gospel in a world where evil forces are in operation will always mean suffering."[53] Is resistance a synonym of Christian obedience? In the context of socio-cultural-economic-political oppression, "Christian obedience as resistance" is a meaningful slogan for the Christian community to speak for the victimised.

---

[50] *Ibid.*, 40-43.

[51] Paulose Mar Paulose, *Spirituality for Struggle*, 57.

[52] Paulose Mar Paulose, *Church's Mission*, 7.

[53] *Ibid.*, 9

Reconciliation

According to Mar Paulose, God is the word for reconciliation; it is not the word for compromise. The New Testament understanding of the way of reconciliation is risky but strong. It is the way of the cross, death and resurrection.[54] Mar Paulose says that the call to reconciliation demands the Church to relate its proclamation and action to contemporary human experiences by sharing deeply the fears and hopes of people and by entering into the conflicts of the time.[55] Here he emphasises the role of the Church in the ministry of reconciliation. If the Church is not able to take bold steps to oppose social injustices and the violation of human rights, it fails in its mission of reconciliation. In the context of human conflicts, domination and search for freedom, Gospel should be a word of liberation as well as a word of reconciliation. Then only it becomes the message of reconciliation.[56] The gospel of freedom that upholds reconciliation cannot be neutral. It creates partisanship towards the poor, the afflicted and the humiliated. The bias towards the poor is not to harass the rich; it is for the liberation of the humanity of both the oppressed and the oppressor. The partisanship of the Gospel acts not in sectarian or separatist manner but out of a comprehensive concern for all.[57] Here reconciliation advocates liberation, humanisation and active participation in the hopes and aspirations of the poor in the society in order to redeem the whole creation. It ultimately aims for the restoration of universal humanhood and dignity. The reality of reconciliation would become visible when oppressed people are recognised as "human beings" in the mainstream of society.

---

[54] Paulose Mar Paulose, *Nisabdharayirikkan Ningalkkenthadhikaram*, 31.

[55] Paulose Mar Paulose, *Spirituality for Struggle*, 58.

[56] *Ibid.*

[57] Paulose Mar Paulose, *Church's Mission*, 11.

Spirituality for Struggle[58]

For Mar Paulose, spirituality is for struggle. His understanding of spirituality is based on the prophetic spirituality of the Old Testament. "Spirituality is the way to approach the awareness of selfhood, and it will be complete only in relation to God and the fellow beings. Christian spirituality can never be seen as that of an isolated individual; but it is corporate and is given and received in a fellowship."[59] Spirituality is to transform nature, society and history. Such spirituality has the spirit of struggle. It is to identify with the aspirations of people and to protest against the evil structures of society. Prophetic spirituality does not encourage foretelling but forth telling. A right vision of the Kingdom of God is an essential ingredient of the spirituality for struggle.[60] Mar Paulose further emphasised that true spirituality is to be exercised by participating with God in the process of transforming the world in justice and love.[61] He saw spirituality as a source of energy and means to identify his selfhood by participating in the struggles and sufferings of society.[62] If spirituality is for struggle, real spirituality can be seen in the life of those who involve in the struggles of people. It could be religious or

---

[58] Paulose Mar Paulose was influenced by M. M. Thomas' concept of 'Spirituality for Combat.' Thomas says that our struggle is not merely against others, but also against ourselves, not against flesh and blood, but against the false spiritualities of the idolatry of race, nation and class, and of the self-righteousness of ideals, which reinforce collective structures of inhumanity and oppression. Any spirituality of righteousness must start with a turning in repentance from idols to the living God and justification by faith. (M. M. Thomas, "Spirituality For Combat," *NCC Review* Vol. CXVI/ No.1 (1996): 52.)

[59] Paulose Mar Paulose, *Spirituality for Struggle*, 83.

[60] Ibid., 84-85.

[61] Ibid., 91.

[62] Paulose Mar Paulose, *Nisabdharayirikkan Ningalkkenthadhikaram*, 23.

secular. A radical shift from self-centered spirituality to struggle-oriented spirituality is needed to establish a transformed society.

Ecumenism

Being an ecumenist, Mar Paulose tried to give a wider meaning to ecumenism, which transcends the unity of churches to the solidarity and reconciliation of the whole creation in God. Ecumenism has to do with *oikoumene*. It is not limited to the Church or Christians alone, but embraces the whole world. In the context of contemporary realities, ecumenism should try to relate two things—the effort to recover unity in our renewed understanding of faith and the participation in the struggles of people for the realisation of their hopes and aspirations. The unity that neglects the hopes of the people is against the vision of Jesus.[63] Mar Paulose proposed 'an Ecumenism of the Gospel' as the need of the time. The ecumenism of Gospel stands for the renewal of ecumenism based on the renaissance of belief in the Gospel of Jesus Christ. This renewal of ecumenism says 'no' to the reduction of the Gospel to the Church, i.e., Church-centered thinking. But it encourages bringing the Gospel to the secular world in order to witness to the inbreaking of the future Kingdom.[64] The proposal of Paulose Mar Paulose calls for a new ecumenical spirit that is rooted in the Gospel and committed to the aspirations of the suffering people. It is with secular movements that the Ecumenism of the Gospel engages in the secular world.

---

[63] Paulose Mar Paulose, *Spirituality for Struggle*, 62-63.

[64] *Ibid.*, 65.

Theological Anthropology[65]

According to Mar Paulose, it is the will of God that human beings come of age. In the modern world, humans take control over themselves. In our scientific and technological world, they claim that they are able to do and look after their affairs. For him, human beings attained their age according to the knowledge of God. God wills this condition of humans. The coming of age for humans has become possible through Jesus Christ. God does not want humans to be the slaves of ignorance and superstitions. But God likes humans to be free from all kinds of bondages. This coming of age does not mean that humans are sinless, perfect beings. But at a particular time or age, human beings are able to take up the responsibility of this world along with God.[66] It can also be interpreted that human beings in the modern world are mature enough to take up the responsibility of responding to the issues of this world and to work for the liberation of the oppressed sections of society. His idea of coming of age is not to reduce the message of Gospel but to show the responsibility of human beings in relation to this world.

Role of Religion in a Secular Society

Mar Paulose affirmed the positive role of religion and its responsibility in a pluralistic society like India. He highlighted the responsibility of religion for the well-being of human

---

[65] The Theological Anthropology of Mar Paulose is the acknowledgement of the scientific and technological progress of human beings. He developed his theological anthropology from the insights of Bonhoeffer's concept of "World Come of Age." In it, Bonhoeffer criticises the tendency of religion to make humans more dependent on God to solve their problems instead of encouraging human capacities. For him, the world has come to the stage where it can stand on itself.

[66] Paulose Mar Paulose, *Nisabdharayirikkan Ningalkkenthadhikaram*, 105-107.

community. For him, religion is not for dominating society but for enabling the formation of a just society. It is not the duty of any religion to dominate society by taking political leadership.[67] But religions have a political role in supporting the struggles of the people. "Today, poor people are challenging religions to participate in their struggles to attain their basic human rights, not any other benefits."[68] Religion can co-operate with any movement irrespective of caste or color to redeem the meaning and purpose of human life. We can call it redemption or liberation or humanisation. To establish justice and peace, the presence of religion in all secular institutions is an important matter to be considered.[69]

Paulose Mar Paulose encouraged the involvement of religion in politics. It has a prophetic role to raise voices against all kinds of injustice and corruption. By this attempt, religion can make politics more people-oriented than party-oriented.[70] He also emphasised that the involvement of religion in politics should be able to uphold human dignity. Through this endeavour, there must be a re-establishment of universal humanhood. In order to elevate politics into human it has to imbibe spirituality at a deeper level.[71] In a democratic country, the role of religion is to promote democracy and to encourage community life in the light of divine justice. To that end, religion should become the servant of the suffering people; it should not remain as the master of society.[72] What makes a

---

[67] Paulose Mar Paulose, *Swathanthryamanu Daivam*, 35.

[68] *Ibid.*, 22.

[69] *Ibid.*, 23-24.

[70] *Ibid.*, 36.

[71] Paulose Mar Paulose, *Nisabdharayirikkan Ningalkkenthadhikaram*, 25.

[72] *Ibid.*, 35.

religion relevant? "A religion becomes relevant if it relinquishes its conservatism, and becomes revolutionary and partakes in the struggle for a new earth and new heaven, by standing up for the oppressed."[73] Mar Paulose envisions a religion that is prophetic, politically responsive, socially committed and always prepared to initiate dialogue with all secular movements. Here the focus of religion shifts from 'other worldly salvation' to 'liberation' in concrete life experiences.

Secularism

Mar Paulose called himself as a theologian of secularism. For him, "secular state means that which is not controlled by religion. The foundation of secular state should not be on any religion, or religious laws or interests or culture. It does not mean that religion has no role in the society. But its role should be fulfilled in the light of divine justice towards humanhood."[74] He identified two basic principles of secularism. The first basic principle of secularism is to protect the fundamental rights of a person. Therefore, the foundation of a secular state is human being who is able to think and act according to his or her conscience. Secondly, the concept of secularism is based on the principle of religious freedom. Religious freedom is an inalienable part of human freedom. It is not for saying and acting anything but for searching the truth and rejecting the untruth.[75] For him, the main reason for the failure of genuine secularism in India is the approach of different religions to safeguard their rights and privileges without serious commitment to universal humanhood.[76] "For

---

[73] *Ibid.*, 143.

[74] Paulose Mar Paulose, *Swathanthriyamanu Daivam*, 171.

[75] Paulose Mar Paulose, *Nisabdharayirikkan Ningalkkenthadhikaram*, 89-90.

[76] *Ibid.*, 96.

the success of secularism what we need is not the absence of religions, but that religions should go back to their liberative values. Secularism is successful in India when the religions uphold their teaching sincerely."[77] In his thinking, Mar Paulose interpreted the responsibility of religions for the success of secularism in a secular state. He envisioned India as a secular state, enriched by the freedom of its citizens and the creative participation of all religions. The principle of secularism confronts the religions to uphold fundamental human rights. In the light of Divine Justice, the vocation of religions is to show the liberative praxis of doctrinal values in secular society.

Religious Fundamentalism

Mar Paulose opted to be a theologian of secularism in the context of the resurgence of religious revivalism and fundamentalism. In the face of religious fundamentalism, he proposed a re-interpretation of religious teachings to retrieve the liberative motif. He criticised the religious laws that created social disharmony and mistrust. For him, a society of religious tolerance and communal harmony can be realised not by imposing religious laws, but by responding to human aspirations and apprehensions meaningfully.[78] Today, we need to re-interpret religious Scriptures and doctrines to find out the liberative strands. Along with this, he also suggested a vision of universal humanhood. Instead of understanding God in the context of present realities, people tend to understand God as the transcendent One, who is less concerned about human issues. They try to see God apart from the hopes and aspirations of their fellow beings.[79] In order to combat

---

[77] *Ibid.*, 70.

[78] Paulose Mar Paulose, *Swathanthryamanu Daivam*, 118.

[79] *Ibid.*, 118-121.

fundamentalism, he suggests that religion should be silent wherever it is to be silent. In religion, the emotional attitude should be replaced by a logical approach. Religious places and pilgrim centres should be used to reveal the relation between human beings come of ages and God's intention and expectations of human beings.[80] The narrow understanding of religious values and the attempt to limit God within the faith communities result in exclusive claims, which breed religious fanaticism in the minds of people. In this situation, religions should affirm life for the establishment of a society where people are not restricted by religious laws and doctrines.

As a theologian, Paulose Mar Paulose built up his theological expressions in the context of the response of the Church to the hopes and aspirations of the people who were struggling under the dehumanising systems in society. He tried to appropriate his faith in relation to the issues of the people. Exposure to different ideological streams and theological constructs shaped his theological thinking in response to the social challenges of his time. In the theological method of Mar Paulose, contextual issues are the base for theologising. Human concerns are interpreted in the light of Scripture to challenge the Church to engage in the struggles of people. With this method, Mar Paulose articulated his theology as a reply to the misapprehension of the ideas of humanisation, secularism, human rights and the mission of the Church. Here God is presented as freedom, who experiences the pain-pathos of people. So, our spirituality is for the struggle to ensure freedom to everyone in all aspects. In a pluralistic context, human freedom is realisable through

---

[80] *Ibid.*, 123-125.

the deliberate involvement of religious institutions and secular movements in the lives of the voiceless and the marginalised. The underlying principle for this attempt is humanisation.

Chapter 6

The Ecclesiology of Paulose Mar Paulose

The Church occupies an important place in the theology of Paulose Mar Paulose. His ecclesiology was an attempt to redefine the mission of the Church in the context of the challenge of the time. On the one hand, he criticised the Church for its tendency to limit its mission within the Christian community. But on the other hand, he affirmed the significance of Church's involvement in the struggles of the people. He further underscored the interaction between the Church and non-Christian traditions and secular movements for creating universal humanhood. The prophetic participation of the Church in politics was also stressed in his theology. In this section, we will try to analyse his ecclesiology.

Church's Mission: Struggle for Justice

The Church in India has been called out to proclaim the Gospel of abundant life in the context of oppression, hunger and other dehumanising systems. This proclamation of abundant life requires a radical commitment to justice and liberation of humans in the name of Jesus. Spiritual emancipation from sin and material emancipation from the demonic political-economic forces are to be considered equally in the liberative proclamation of the Church.[1]

"The Church is not only a useable tool but a powerful and important tool in God's revolutionary strategy."[2] The struggle for justice is part of the Church's ministry because God wants to create a society where we exercise our full human rights. The struggle for justice is not only for political rights, but also for social and economic rights.[3] He also reminded that in the struggle for justice, the primary task of the Church is to be God's people in this world. In this attempt, the Church of Jesus should proclaim the Gospel with all its liberating implications and interpret the Gospel, not to maintain the status quo and a policy that preserve the vested interests, but to come out of its state of stagnation.[4] In the struggle for justice, the role of the Church is not limited to the proclamation of the Gospel alone. But the Church is challenged to identify "with those who have become the victims of oppression, exploitation and slavery and are forced to live a second class life in poverty and hunger, and join them in their struggle for justice. If we refuse to help them, that means, we refuse to participate in the suffering of God."[5]

---

[1] Paulose Mar Paulose, "Indian Christian Theology, the Church and the People." *Religion and Society* Vol.XXX / No 384 (September-December, 1983): 87.

[2] Paulose Mar Paulose, *Church's Mission* (Bombay: BUILD, n.d.),2

[3] *Ibid.*

[4] Paulose Mar Paulose, *Spirituality for Struggle* (Thiruvalla: CSS, 1999), 27-28.

[5] Paulose Mar Paulose, *Church's Mission*, 6.

In the struggles for justice, Mar Paulose observed that the Church can become a powerful tool in God's revolutionary strategy only if it is ready to participate in the suffering of God in the world. The suffering of God in this world is evident in the contemporary struggles of the people for justice. At the same time, when the Church fails to stand by the poor, it becomes the religion of the rich and the powerful sections of society.[6] So, Mar Paulose proposed the partisanship of the Church with the poor, the afflicted and the humiliated. In this partisanship, the hopes and aspirations of the voiceless groups are to be upheld. Here, instead of fighting for our own rights and privileges, we need to strive for the dignity and rights of the wider community.[7] Jesus accomplished his work of liberation by standing on the side of the outcastes by accepting the so-called ungodly people and by helping the needy and the sick. This is the rationale for the concept of "Partisanship with the Poor." So, the Church is called to respond to the issues of those who are deprived of justice, peace and human rights. It demands participation in their struggles.[8] The struggles for justice then become the mission of the Church because Church's mission is Jesus' mission. The "Partisanship with Poor" invites the Church to involve in the struggles of people who are affected by the establishment of Special Economic Zones, and of the Dalits and Adivsis who are deprived of their rights. Here the Church's mission for justice is to materialise God's revolutionary strategy—the liberation of the entire creation. For that, the Church needs to see the suffering of God in the pain-pathos of fellow beings who experience poverty, discrimination and inhuman treatment.

---

[6] *Ibid.*, 10-11.

[7] Paulose Mar Paulose, *Spirituality for Struggle*, 29.

[8] *Ibid.*, 55.

Church's Mission: Involvement in Political Struggles

Paulose Mar Paulose believed that the Church has to bear witness in the political realm as well. For him, the Church's mission also included the involvement of the Church in various political struggles. Involvement in politics does not necessarily mean to join political parties. He was vehemently against the communalisation of politics. So, he never advocated Christians to join the political parties for communal interests. The Church's political witness simply means Church's participation in the ongoing struggles of the time to transform radically the prevailing sinful social relations:

> The response of love toward God and the neighbor requires participation in the political process. Along with other citizens, Christians have responsibility to confront, understand, and attempt to solve the problems like providing food for hungry, alleviating poverty and unemployment; grappling with deadly issues like environmental pollution; finding ways to control the population explosion; and building up a world of peace with justice.[9]

To participate actively in politics, the Church should encourage and train its members. The political participation of the Church is through its members. The Church's involvement in the political process means that every Church member must understand his or her place as Christ's witness in everyday life. Each member signifies the presence of the Church in society.[10]

It is also important here to recognise that Mar Paulose was against the communal politics of the Indian Church. In the name of minority rights, instead of striving for establishing the rights of the entire human family, the Indian Church is

---

[9] Paulose Mar Paulose, *Church's Mission*, 12.

[10] *Ibid.*, 15.

striving to protect its own rights and privileges. Unless and until their interests are not endangered, the churches do not encourage the people to participate in the political process. But once their interests are in danger, they encourage political participation to safeguard minority rights.[11] Mar Paulose views that in the political struggles, the Church should give priority to the struggles of the marginalised. Moreover, the Church is not qualified to proclaim the Gospel if it does not participate in the sufferings and hopes of the society and identify with the marginalised. The Gospel always compels the Church to stand for the afflicted and to side with the oppressed in their struggles.[12] Here the decisive factor is not the numerical strength of the Church but its readiness to suffer with God in the world.[13] Therefore, the Church cannot be neutral in its approach. The Church must "have a preferential option for" the oppressed and the downtrodden. The political involvement of the Church is not to safeguard the rights of the Christian community, but to witness as a powerful tool in God's revolutionary strategy. It is for recognising the dignity and the rights of human beings, and we can do it only through joining in their struggles. Ultimately, political participation in the struggles for justice means participation in the suffering of God in human life.

The Church and Human beings "Coming of Age"

Human beings coming of age is a unique affirmation in the theology of Paulose Mar Paulose. In the context of scientific and technological development, human beings are in a position to take decisions and to carry out their responsibilities

---

[11] Paulose Mar Paulose, *Nisabdharayirikkan Ningalkkenthadhikaram (Mal)* (Noorannad: Fabian Books, 1998), 42.

[12] *Ibid.*, 31.

[13] Paulose Mar Paulose, *Spirituality for Struggle*, 41-42.

by themselves. In such a situation, Mar Paulose explored the role of the Church in relation to human beings coming of age. He provided some guidelines in that direction. Firstly, the great task of the Church at present is to make the world know the "human beings coming of age" and the divine purpose of them; and the Church must be the venue for this. Secondly, as the Church and individuals, we are called to create an atmosphere where human beings can live as humans. The rationale behind this approach is, in Jesus Christ, God became a human, not a Christian. So, it is the responsibility of the Church to identify the God-given potential in human beings, to bring out the truth in them and to encourage them to participate in the renewal activities of God in this world. Thirdly, the Church's activities of charity and justice should be balanced. The Church is liable to send Red-Cross volunteers to war-affected regions; it is also committed to condemn and stop war. Fourthly, the Church's activities of charity and justice should be based on Christian hope. Fifthly, since God is for all, He may speak and reveal through people of other faiths, secular movements and our neighbours. So the Church should engage in dialogue with other faiths and ideologies. It may help the Church to evaluate whether it strives to create harmonious life in society. Finally, the Church should oppose the governments that support communalism and interpret minority rights in the light of wider human rights.[14] Here the Church must ask bold questions, such as How many people or groups enjoy freedom to stand by themselves in the midst of oppressive systems? Whether scientific and technological potentials are directed to the upliftment of the 'least ones' in society?

---

[14] *Ibid.*, 111-114.

The Church and the State

Human communities are created with a divine purpose. That should be realised in the framework of society. It means the divine purpose has to be materialised, not by rejecting the social nature of humans but by recognising it.[15] So, Mar Paulose suggested that it is the responsibility of the Church and the Christians to evaluate whether a community or system works for the realisation of the divine purpose or creates hindrance to the welfare of humans. In this sense, the interests of the Church are spread out in all realms of society. The State is also included in it. The State is a divine gift.[16] It is an instrument to fulfill the divine purpose on individuals, society and state. Here the role of the Church is to observe the activities of the State; whether it works for the welfare of humanity or not. The Church's involvement in the affairs of the State is not for establishing minority rights and privileges, but for realising the purpose of God in this world.[17] Mar Paulose also understood the Church as a corrective force when the State goes against the interests of the people. The Church should consider resistance as a form of Christian obedience when people are denied justice. Human welfare is the aim of any government. When the State fails in this mission, it automatically negates the divine purpose. So, the responsibility of the Church is to resist the State when it becomes a means of oppression.[18] In the light of Divine justice, the Church has a prophetic role in motivating the State to fulfill

---

[15] Paulose Mar Paulose, *Swathanthryamanu Daivam (Mal.)* (Ariyannur: Patabhedam, 1996), 89.

[16] It is possible that Mar Paulose was influenced by Bonhoeffer's understanding of the State as Divinely ordained authority and in its being; it is a divine office. (Dietrich Bonhoeffer, *Ethics*, 297 & 305)

[17] Paulose Mar Paulose, *Swathanthryamanu Daivam*, 90-91.

[18] *Ibid.*, 93.

the divine purpose—the welfare of all citizens. The Church should also make use of its influence to speak for the people who are denied justice.

The Church and the Secular Society

Secularism is another important category in the theology of Mar Paulose. He opposed religious fundamentalism and affirmed religious plurality as a divine gift. He upheld the universal humanhood and liberative values of different religions. Mar Paulose believed that the Church has a significant role in creating and protecting the secular society in our pluralistic context. He identified six important points that the Church in India has to take seriously in its approach to secular society. Firstly, in order to defeat communalism and to encourage secularism, the Church should become united for the cause of the weak and the voiceless over against its interests in the name of minority rights. Secondly, the Church's control and domination in society should be reduced. The Church can encourage society spiritually and morally through individuals only when it consciously keeps away from the centre of power. Thirdly, Christian ecumenism should not be a hindrance to the unity of the entire human community. It means that churches should respond to the common issues of society. Fourthly, the Church must encourage and support the secular ideologies that are directed to the welfare of human community. Fifthly, churches should co-operate with Social Action Groups that are working for socio-economic and political justice. Finally, the Church should resist the governments that foster communalism and must understand the minority rights in the light of human rights. Here the matter is, whether the Church is willing to stand along with human society.[19] By highlighting the Church's role in secular

---

[19] Paulose Mar Paulose, *Nisabdharayirikkan Ningalkkenthadhikaram*, 101-103.

society, Mar Paulose emphasised a society that is not controlled by any religion and exhorted the Church to participate with other religious and secular movements to create a just society.

The Church and Globalisation

Mar Paulose was critical about globalisation and he attempted to enable the Church to be a prophetic witness in the context of neo-liberal invasion. His response to globalisation can be summarised in five points. Firstly, the Church should stand for the rights of the people to reject the dominant development model that is imposed upon them. Secondly, the Church must have a prophetic voice against the accumulation of wealth that creates inequality in society. Thirdly, the Church is responsible for the development of society but needs to be ready to denounce the bad-effects of development due to globalisation. Fourthly, the Church should take initiative to encourage appropriate technologies and to discourage technologies or industries that are harmful to the creation; for example, militarisation. Fifthly, our freedom and self-determination should not be submitted to wealthy nations. For that, the Church must conscientise the people about what is needed for human welfare and must enable them to have the willpower to attain it.[20] The above-mentioned guiding principles must lead the Church to join in the issues of the victims of globalisation. The Special Economic Zones, the IT corridors and the like, the offsprings of globalisation, cause many poor people to be dispossessed of their own lands. They get a meagre amount as land price from the concerned authorities. The entrance of multi-national companies into retail trade badly affects the prospects of the small-scale business community. Farmers do not get enough value for their goods in globalised markets. In this context, the Church should

---

[20] Paulose Mar Paulose, *Swathanthryamanu Daivam*, 163-165.

unite with the farmers, the evicted people and the poor merchants in their protests to resist the forces of globalisation.

The Church and Minority Rights

The Christian community is an organised minor part of the Indian society. They have possession of a large portion of educational institutions. They make use of their political influence to accomplish community interests in localities where they are dominant. They often uphold the minority status to establish their rights on various issues. In the name of minority rights, they enjoy the privileges and are less concerned with the human rights issues of other communities, especially the oppressed. In such a context, Mar Paulose proposed a new definition of the term minority community and explained minority rights in the context of human rights. He interpreted minority status in relation to the communities that experience marginalisation and oppression. In his thinking, the Church was not a minority community. "Religion is not the criterion to decide who is minority and who is majority. Minority group means a people who are disempowered. In this sense, the term minority refers to the people who are oppressed, poor, voiceless and powerless in the society. So the minority-majority distinction has to be made on the basis of power relations."[21] He also observed that in fact the majority is being oppressed by the minority, who holds power and wealth. So the majority should unite and resist this minority. The majority-minority distinction based on religion may only benefit the interests of the elites of respective religions.[22] Mar Paulose was critical of the Church for using minority rights to bargain for their rights and privileges. In

---

[21] Paulose Mar Paulose, *Nisabdharayirikkan Ningalkkenthadhikaram*, 41.

[22] *Ibid.*

this aspect, he suggested that minority rights should not be used only to manage schools, colleges and hospitals for financial gains. It cannot be considered as religious dharma.[23]

Mar Paulose was not against the minority rights granted to the Indian Church by the constitution. His criticism emerged as a reaction to the Church's overemphasis on minority rights to safeguard its rights and privileges without commitment to the poor and the weak. For him, the Church should combine its activities for minority rights and human rights. The logic behind this approach is, Jesus was born in a minority situation in his context. He never stood for minority privileges. But he worked for human rights. In this way, Christians in India have to ask minority rights not as part of the Christian minority condition but as part of each citizen's fundamental human rights.[24] Mar Paulose identified two dangers in the minority consciousness of the Indian Church. Firstly, the Church and the Christians are often not interested in the affairs of the country and often afraid to get involved in the socio-political and economic struggles for social justice. Secondly, the Church is too concerned about its own rights and privilege and not about the rights and privilege of the human community outside the Church.[25] Here the intention of Mar Paulose was to bring in radical changes in the priorities of the Church within the community to the wider human society. The Church in India can enjoy minority rights only in the name of Jesus. Since Jesus stood for the rights of all, the Church, the community of Jesus, cannot be a mute spectator to the aspirations of other communities.

---

[23] *Ibid.*, 68.

[24] Ibid., 86-87.

[25] Paulose Mar Paulose, *Spirituality for Struggle*, 24-26.

The Church and Human Rights

All through his life, Mar Paulose was much concerned about the protection of human rights. He even interpreted the minority rights in the light of human rights. In his understanding, the Church is called to protect the rights of all people irrespective of religion and ideology. For him, the Church is forced to think about human rights because God so loved this world; and so we are also accountable for loving this world.[26] He proposed three things that need to be considered when the Church works for human rights. Firstly, the Church should evaluate itself whether it acts as a force of injustice in the world or not. Here the Church needs to understand the needs of the people and evaluate whether it stands to respond to those needs or not. Secondly, the Church should be a model in society for creating progressive transformations; it must be a community without economic disparity, violence and injustice. Thirdly, the Church cannot be silent in the face of human rights violations, because Jesus represented God's confrontation with the forces of dehumanisation.[27] Here Mar Paulose reminds us that struggle for human rights cannot be separated from the ministry of the Church. The Church's mission for human rights envisions a society where all are free and all experience the God-given rights with mutual responsibility.

As a powerful instrument in the revolutionary strategy of God, the Church is called to struggle along with the people who are deprived of justice, rights, dignity and humanhood. It reminds the Christian community to have well-focused attempts to realise the liberative vision of God. The Church should take bold steps to protect the rights and privileges of

---

[26] Paulose Mar Paulose, *Swathanthryamanu Daivam*, 97.

[27] *Ibid.*, 101-104.

all people groups irrespective of faith and community affiliations. The Church should become a platform for listening to the voice of the 'no-people.' The involvement of the Church in the wretched life realities of people would certainly enable the faith community to experience God, who defends the cause of the entire creation. As a prophetic voice, the Church cannot be neutral in fighting against life-negating forces. In sum, the ecclesiology of Paulose Mar Paulose affirms life in its fullness.

Chapter 7

The Political Witness of the Church in India: A Theological Appraisal

God of Struggle: The Source of Political Witness

Paulose Mar Paulose claims that the distinctive feature of Christianity is that God whom the Christians worship is the one who suffered with humanity and still participates in the suffering of His creation.[1] This God leads all the revolutions of the time for the preservation of human dignity and prosperity. So, the Church cannot say that we are not interested in politics. Here politics can be understood as political struggles in society.[2]

---

[1] Paulose Mar Paulose, *Vithakyappetta Vithukal* (Malayalam) Collection by K.J. Thomas (Trissur: Paulose Mar Paulose Foundation for Socio-Cultural Development, 2005), 78.

[2] Paulose Mar Paulose, *Swathanthryamanu Daivam* (Malayalam) (Ariyannur: Patabhedam, 1996), 92.

This God can be met authentically in the ongoing struggles of the people who are striving to establish their human rights. The incarnation of this God in Jesus Christ through the revolutionary intervention in society broke the caste system, made the socio-cultural religious customs subservient to higher values and attacked the religious institutionalism that supported injustices.[3] The God of struggle cannot be limited to the rites and sacrament of the Church. He is beyond the traditions and creedal definitions of the Church. The participation of God in the struggles of people is not to keep creation as passive sufferers but to renew everything in the world.[4] Here the derived notion is that the source of political witness of the Church is God who struggles along with humans to renew the whole creation. So, political witness is to renew society by helping the poor and the marginalised to enjoy freedom, equality and human dignity. As the Church worships the God of struggle, its political witness should be the witness of struggle.

In today's context, the Church should be able to see God in the protests of people whose life is threatened by socio-economic-political forces. The followers of Jesus must realise the fact that the location of God in this world is the life of the downtrodden ones in society. It may be the Dalits who are humiliated because of caste identity, or the Tribals who suffer because of land alienation or the women who struggle to get equal status in social life or the people who are under utter poverty or subaltern people groups whose livelihood is disturbed due to Special Economic Zones, etc. Since God is intentionally engaged in the life realities of these people, the

---

[3] Paulose Mar Paulose, *Spirituality for Struggle* (Thiruvalla: CSS, 1999), 40.

[4] Paulose Mar Paulose, *Nisabdharayirikan Ningalkkenthadhikaram?* (Malayalam) (Nooranad: Fabian Books, 1998), 109.

responsibility of the Church is to discover Him and to participate in the renewal and liberative mission of God. Therefore, in a democratic pluralistic situation, the Church can make use of its political witness for intervening in the desperate condition of the people to celebrate life in its fullness. By this attempt, on the one hand, the Church experiences theophany and on the other hand, the Church can show that God who was revealed in Jesus is not a communal God but rather a God who can understand the pain of the entire creation.

Ecumenism: A Unity for Solidarity with Poor

Ecumenism is understood as unity of churches for the welfare of Christian community. It focuses on the relationship of different churches to stand for the common cause. Ecumenism in India is often strengthened to fight against the State or to establish the privileges, or to uphold the issues related to the Christian community. The concerns of ecumenism in the pluralistic context are limited to the interests of believers only. The approach of ecumenism sometimes seems to be communal in nature. It seldom raises the issues of the people of other faiths. Mar Paulose observes that ecumenism is not restricted to the Church or Christians alone; it embraces the whole world. It should try to relate both the effort to recover unity in our renewed understanding of faith and the participation in the struggles of the people for realisation of their hopes and aspirations. The unity that neglects the hopes of people is against the vision of Jesus.[5] It implies that real ecumenism is intended to respond to contemporary human realities irrespective of religio-cultural-ethnic identities. It directly points to the active involvement of churches in the efforts of the oppressed masses to reclaim social justice. The wider

---

[5] Paulose Mar Paulose, *Spirituality for Struggle*, 62-63.

ecumenism that includes people of other faiths and no faiths helps the Church to accomplish the same. This wider ecumenism can be called, as M. M. Thomas puts it, 'secular koinonia', where the Church can participate actively in the efforts to protect life. It is not like the ecumenism of Kerala churches with caste organisations to protect their interests without hearing the cry of the underprivileged ones in society. But today's ecumenism has become unity for communal interest than unity for empowering the downtrodden people. The Church never speaks out as an ecumenical entity for the weaker sections of the society, including Dalit Christians.

Ecumenism in India becomes theologically valid if it addresses the vital issues of society because involvement in human struggles is the prophetic vision of Jesus. It must call the people to work for the elimination of economic and social injustice. It should support the Government for the programmes that are aimed to help the people under the poverty line. The ecumenism of the Church must see the plight of poor farmers in the country, reject communal politics and raise voice for the people who lost their land because of development projects. Instead of arguing for sectarian interests, ecumenism must be used to engage with the actual life situation and to participate in the movements of protest. In the context of ecumenism, the political witness of the Church is to join hands with secular movements to work for human development.

Spirituality for Political Witness

For Mar Paulose Christian spirituality is for struggle. It is based on the Old Testament prophetic spirituality. It is a corporeal experience and is meant for transforming society. Such spirituality identifies with the hopes and fears of people and protests against the evil structures of society. So, it is clear that spirituality is to struggle for establishing a transformed society and to participate in the very fact of human experiences of the time. The basic foundation for spirituality for struggle is the vision of Kingdom of God.[6] This spirituality can be interpreted in the contemporary context as spirituality for political witness. Here spirituality is strongly affirmed for the political witness that can bring changes in the life of millions of people. Political witness is constructive and prophetic, for it transforms the community and opposes evil tendency. Spirituality for political witness is not sectarian but communitarian, where life is the point of departure. The political witness of the Church cannot be blind to social realities, because concern for others is the foundation of genuine spirituality. Spirituality for political witness affirms that God is in the process of renewing the world. So, the political witness of the Church cannot move away from the sufferings of society. Spirituality for political witness, life-affirming spirituality through struggle, can be seen in the life of those who stand for the voiceless, the powerless and the marginalised. It reminds the Christian community that spirituality becomes reality when it confronts the life of others. It demands the shift of focus from the interests of the Christian community to the wider human community.

Spirituality for political witness reveals the fact that the spirituality of the Church gets its authenticity in its support to the political struggles of the people. The spirituality of the Church gets a new meaning and becomes the source of energy for liberation when the Church attacks the power structures supported by unjust means. In the context of economic exploitation and social oppressive structures, the spirituality that inspires people to fight against dehumanising power relations is the need of the hour for the Church. Therefore, the spirituality for political witness demands the Church to

---

[6] *Ibid.*, 83-85.

partake in the life of subaltern people whose voice is suppressed. It is not to establish comfort zones but to be with people who are pushed aside to live as second-class citizens. Though it contains an element of risk, the Church can try to turn the spirituality that is centred on individual pietism into spirituality that is responsive to social issues. In spirituality, the place of human life is higher than ritualistic observances.

Role of Religion: Liberative Politics, Not Communal Politics

Communalism and religious fundamentalism are two major threats to Indian secular society. Religion is often misused by politicians to maintain their political agenda and power. In fact, religion is an important element in the life of Indian people, especially in the political realm. In his theology, Mar Paulose highlights the role of religion in politics. He understands religion in relation to the welfare of community. He negates the role of religion in taking political leadership. But he affirms the engagement of religion in politics to raise voice against injustice, corruption, influence of money and caste, wrong priorities of the State, etc. The basis for such engagement is human dignity. For him, the political role of religions is to support the struggles of people to attain their basic human rights.[7] These insights lead to the point that the role of religion is to promote liberative politics, not communal politics. In communal politics, the interests of a particular group is protected and encouraged, whereas in liberative politics, the agenda of political witness is the well-being of the entire community. In liberative politics, people are the centre of political activity, whereas in communal politics, it is the vested interests of the rich and powerful who dominate the political sphere. Liberative politics is prophetic and

---

[7] Paulose Mar Paulose, *Swathanthryamanu Daivam*; 35, 22-24 & 36.

responsive to human issues. Communal politics is defensive and creates hatred and enmity among communities. In liberative politics, religion is used as a corrective force to transform society; in communal politics, religion is misused to polarise society for political mileage.

Does the Church promote liberative politics or communal politics? It is an undeniable fact that the Church understands its political witness as liberative, while an outsider will observe it as communal because the Church's struggle is only for its own rights and privileges. In this context, the political witness of the Church should bring liberation to the people who challenge their oppressors for humanhood and human dignity. So, the Church has only one option, i.e., identify with the movements of liberation for affirming human life. If it does not address the apprehensions of human beings, irrespective of faith and tradition, the witness of the Church automatically becomes communal. Liberative politics reminds the Church to be prophetic in all aspects of social life. It has the responsibility to analyse human-life realities in the light of divine justice. The Church cannot be silent to human issues if it upholds liberative politics in society.

Minority Rights: The Rights to Serve Society

Mar Paulose understood minority rights in the light of human rights. In the context of the Church's overemphasis on the minority rights guaranteed by the constitution, he interpreted them in relation to the people who are deprived of basic human rights. In his thinking, Mar Paulose emphasised that marginalised communities need special privilege to come up in society. For him, minority group means people who are disempowered in all aspects of life. It implies that minority groups are oppressed, poor, voiceless and powerless communities. The minority understanding of Mar Paulose must be understood in the light of the objectives of minority privileges. He was also critical of the Church for using minority rights to protect their interests without any concern for the weaker sections of the people who need such privileges to be empowered themselves. The crux of Mar Paulose's argument is that minority rights are given to empower the whole community.[8] In the context of the debate on minority rights, K. T. Thomas, former Supreme Court judge, says that "minority rights are not to be claimed as privileges; rather they should be taken as a protection offered by the constitution. And no one is to claim these as one's rights forgetting the responsibilities..."[9] These insights lead to the assumption that minority rights are to serve the whole community irrespective of religious traditions and to uplift the downtrodden.

How does the Church, a minority community in India, respect the inner spirit of minority rights? In today's society, the Church's political witness has been protecting minority rights and those rights are used to start educational institutions, which are not accessible to common people. The Church often forgets the fact that its privileges are given to transform and enrich the social, cultural and political realms of the nation. It understands minority rights as a communal privilege. It is evident in the attempts of the churches in Kerala against the Kerala Professional Colleges Bill and Kerala Educational Reforms. They challenged the implementation of reservation in self-financing colleges and the proposal to make appointments through Public Service Commission. The Church opposes such radical efforts by overlooking its

---

[8] Paulose Mar Paulose, *Nisabdharayirikkan Ningalkkenthadhikaram*, 41, 68, & 86-87.

[9] K .T. Thomas, "Not an Article of Special Privilege but Only a Provision for Protection," Reported by R. C. Thomas, *People's Reporter* Vol. 19/No.14 (July 25-August 10, 2006): 1.

responsibility to protect the poor subaltern people who are not able to get quality education because of the unbearable fees structure. If the Church is not able to make available the benefits of minority rights to the wider community, it stands against the hopes and aspirations of the underprivileged to whom Jesus proclaimed the gospel of life. Here the basic problem is the Church's self-understanding as a communal entity that is against the spirit of ecclesia.

Chapter 8
Political Witness: A Journey of Affirming Life

Political Witness: Theological Foundation

Theology is 'life-talk' It is an encounter of life with faith and an attempt to understand and reflect faith in the light of life-realities. In political witness, theologising comes out of conscious response to the issues faced by people. It implies an act of encountering and identifying with the people whose life is disturbed by various oppressive systems in society. Political witness is theologising because it is not simply 'reflecting' but an intentional engagement with God in human life realities under the dominant forces that negate life. In such a theological endeavour, the agenda of the Church is not communal interests but human welfare. Political witness means supporting the voiceless, the socially neglected and the politically disempowered. In political witness, faith-talk interacts with suffering people and Theology becomes Theo-praxis. Political witness as theologising affirms human dignity, makes human beings aware of their situation and motivates them to raise voice against the dehumanising systems of society. It serves those who are in the struggles to safeguard their rights and privileges. In this sense, political witness lives out Jesus' mission. Political witness can be defined as theological praxis, where faith is translated into action.

Through political witness, a theological attempt is made to oppose discriminatory attitudes and to correct the erroneous priorities of the State and society. It is a theological act, because God is present in all the attempts that are for the prosperity of humanity. It is also notable that Christ whose form is Church is present in all human struggles. By participating in the political struggles for justice, the Church is participating in the suffering of God in society. The Christ who is present in the human struggle for justice can be demonstrated to the world through the Church's involvement in the political struggles of the oppressed and the marginalised.

Political Witness: A Sacramental Act

The word 'sacramental' refers to the practice that expresses the faith of the Church. Through sacraments, people express their concrete faith. Since political witness refers to the act of involvement in the struggles of the least ones in society, by doing so, the Church proclaims the faith that Jesus Christ is with the suffering people and that his life was for human liberation from the clutches of dehumanisation. Political witness becomes sacramental when the faith community expresses its faith by raising voice for the voiceless, empowering the powerless and questioning the structures of oppression. The rationale behind this sacramentality of political witness is Jesus' intentional encounter with human realities and his relentless effort to establish kingdom values. Today's political witness of the Church becomes a sacramental act if the Church is willing to move with the people who protest to establish gender equality, Dalit rights, land rights and human dignity. As a sacramental act, political witness can be identified with Baptism and Eucharist. Political witness is the Baptism of the Church in the life of fellow human beings whose life is neglected in society. By this baptism, the identity of the Church will emerge more as a community for others than a communal entity. As faith community identifies with the sufferings of Jesus through the sacrament of baptism so political witness enables the Church to involve in the pain-pathos of poor beings in whom Jesus is present. Political witness is also Eucharist because the Church participates in the sufferings of people, which symbolises Jesus' wretched agony. On the one hand, it helps the Church to evoke the suffering image of Jesus; on the other hand, it becomes the means of sharing the broken body of Jesus with the despised ones—those who are denied justice, freedom and equality. As a Eucharist, political witness of the Church is done with the hope of liberation and transformation. Political witness as a sacramental act takes the sacrament outside the Church to give life to all.

Political Witness: A Foretaste of the Reign of God

The Church is known as a community of eschatological hope. The promise and expectation of the Kingdom of God is the actual strength of eschatological hope.[1] The mission of the Church is also understood in the framework of eschatological hope. For Moltmann, "the mission takes place within its own peculiar horizon of the eschatological expectation of the coming kingdom of God, of the coming righteousness and the coming peace, of the coming freedom and human dignity."[2] The main concern of Jesus was also the reign of God. He lived in the hope that God would come to rule over the

---

[1] Jurgen Moltmann, *Theology of Hope* (London: SCM Press Ltd, 1967), 216.

[2] *Ibid.*, 327.

world (Mt.1:15).[3] It is to be noted that the Church exists on the basis of eschatological hope and tries to experience the kingdom in this world through various means. Here political witness stands as a foretaste of the reign of God because it strives hard to bring transformation in society. Moreover, through its involvement in the life of people, political witness opens new horizons of liberation. Thus, eschatological hope is realised on earth. Political witness upholds kingdom values and gives hope of freedom and justice to those who are struggling to celebrate their life. It lives out the eschatological hope imbibed in creeds and faith affirmations and makes the reign of God visible in society. It reminds the faith community that eschatological hope becomes reality through its engagement with the concerns of the marginalised. The Nazareth manifesto of Jesus validates this position. In sum, restoration of humanhood, a foretaste of the kingdom, is the spirit of political witness.

Political Witness: Celebration of Life

Political witness is a celebration of life because it is a life-affirming activity. It intervenes in the life of struggling people to empower them to enjoy a life of freedom and dignity. The foundation of this assertion is God of prophetic tradition who revealed the value of life. Human life is God given, and every human life is the image of God. The underlying principle behind political witness as a celebration of life is Jesus who participated in the struggles of people to celebrate their life. The importance of human life can be understood in the life and work of Jesus. Since God became human in Jesus to save human life, it is human responsibility to protect and celebrate life in its fullness. Celebration of life is the right of every human being, as all are created to enjoy that life. But in the midst of

---

[3] S. Kappen, *Jesus and Society* (Delhi: ISPCK, 2002), 133.

life-negating structures and situations, political witness attempts to see God in the life of people who are not able to celebrate their life. It empowers the disempowered sections to enjoy their life in society. Moreover, wherever life is celebrated, it is also the celebration of the Gospel because the Gospel is the proclamation of life. The political witness of the Indian Church becomes a celebration of life if it leads the marginalised to a life of equality, justice and freedom. In this attempt, the location and vocation of the Church are human beings and their life condition. Since political witness is a celebration of life in community, the Church must join hands with any group that is committed to humanisation. It implies that the Church's existence is for celebration of life through its intervention in socio-political-economic-religious realms. The celebration within the Church becomes meaningless unless and until life is celebrated outside the faith community. Political witness helps the Church of faith to become the community of life. It challenges people to transform their faith into 'life affirming power' that works for celebration of life.

Alternative Form of Being the Church in India

Church: The Jesus Community

The Church in a pluralistic context cannot be a communal society because it is a worldly reality for all people irrespective of religious identities. As Bonhoeffer emphasised, it is the Christ-existing community that exists for the entire humanity and the form of Jesus on earth that engage with the issues faced by people. Moreover, the Church is called to struggle for people who are deprived of justice and to be concerned with the issues faced by the wider human community. Therefore, the Church can be called as the Jesus Community that stands for justice. As Community of Jesus, its focus is to engage with the life realities of human beings rather than to become a custodian of creeds and traditions. It is to raise voices for the suffering humanity and to encounter the diverse experiences of people. The Church as Jesus Community is not separate from Jesus Christ. As Sebastian Kappen emphasised, the disciples of Jesus must stay with Jesus, i.e., "share his faith, his hope and his destiny."[4] Therefore, it has to follow in the footsteps of Jesus in carrying out its mission. It implies that the Jesus Community cannot be a mute spectator of today's socio-political-religious realities in the pluralistic society. The present communal identity of the Church can be replaced by the Community of Jesus. It happens when the Church exists for the concerns of all people as Jesus did. It means that the Church must be ready to hear the cries of the oppressed in the Indian plural context. It should take concentrated action and should have the determination to fight against unjust economic and political systems. By doing so, the Church would be known as the Jesus Community that stands more for celebration of life than for communal interests. If the Jesus Community does not counter structural sins, it would be an "institutionalized betrayal of Jesus."[5]

The Church in the pluralistic context must have dialogue and action-oriented relationships with secular movements. They should be considered not as threat but as partners in mission. The theology and faith of the Jesus Community in the pluralistic context becomes dynamic when it engages with various religio-secular ideologies and traditions in society. In the predicament of communal identity, the Church should go back to its true nature, i.e., the Jesus Community. It should be prophetic, politically responsible and socially committed to understanding the issues faced by people. The Church in a pluralistic society must affirm that social issues are the issues of the Church.

---

[4] *Ibid.,* 137.

[5] *Ibid.,* 140.

The Church: Community of Subaltern Consciousness

The Indian Church is more aware of its minority consciousness. It fails to remember that it is the subaltern groups who need the service of the 'Servant Church.' The Church as the Community of Jesus must primarily concentrate on the rights of the subaltern people who are disempowered socially, economically and religiously. In the context of overemphasis on minority rights, the Church should re-think about who the real minority groups are in the light of human rights. The Church of the present context must become the community of subaltern consciousness, which is rooted in the commitment to the well-being of millions of people who are striving to establish their rights and privileges. The foundation of this subaltern consciousness is Jesus, who is in solidarity with the painful experiences of the least ones in society. It is the responsibility of the so-called 'minority' Church to work for the unorganised majority—the powerless people. The issues of Adivasis, Dalits, Tribals and other subaltern communities and women should be the concerns of the Church today. The political witness of such community is to combat the vicious forces that make people objects in the hands of exploitative structures. Identification with the struggles and aspirations of marginalised sections within and outside the Church is the hallmark of the Church as a community of subaltern consciousness. It goes beyond the vision of an institutional, structural and hierarchical form of Church.

Communal consciousness distorts the witness of the Church in a pluralistic context, which is susceptible in all dimensions. In such a situation, the witness of the Church is also to live out its vocation for the liberation of people who are outside the faith community. The political witness of the Church is an important tool to participate in the life of fellow beings who are still longing for freedom and humanhood. Theological self-understanding of the Church narrows down the scope of the political witness of the Church. The locus of political witness consists of those who are exploited and denied fuller life. Political witness is a theological act in which God of struggle is the base for responding to the issues of society. Spirituality of the faith community must be motivated for political witness to transform the life of others. Theological insights into political witness lead to a redefinition of the Church as the Jesus Community and the Community of subaltern consciousness.

Conclusion

The Church and its mission have always been understood differently. Theologians have articulated the nature and vocation of the Church theologically. The challenges and needs of people in a particular context largely influence the witness of the faith community. The Church as a community of liberative faith and witness should not be understood as a communal entity. It has the larger vision of integral liberation of the entire humanity, a vision beyond the four walls of the Christian community. It has to bear the spirit of Jesus' mission in its fuller sense. Therefore, the locus of its witness is human beings and their life-realities. Indeed, the witness of the Church is to transform society. In witnessing, the Church is living out its faith in the midst of contemporary challenges. However, often the witness of the Church fails to address the interests of our neighbours. This dilemma is evident in the political witness of the Church in India today.

The ecclesiology of Dietrich Bonhoeffer affirms that the Church is the manifestation of Christ's presence in the world. It implies that the Church is the beacon of healing, justice and peace. It is a channel of celebrating Christ's presence in the context of broken life realities. It is to be noted that the Church becomes Christ's real presence if it exists for all people irrespective of faith and community affiliations. This is the mandate of the Church given by Jesus Christ. It is not a communal entity, but a community of Jesus that encounters the world realities of this generation. It is a community of liberating people from the bondage of sinful structures and relations. Therefore, in a pluralistic democratic context, the Church cannot ignore the political activity of the State. It should actively involve in the political life of the nation to engage with the issues of people. The political engagement of the Church in society is for affirming life in its richness. It has responsibility to stand for the cause of others and to help emerge a responsible nation.

As a corrective force, the Church's role is to deliberately involve in all aspects of community life. It has to live out its faith to respond to the spiritual and community needs of the people. For that, the Church should stand against all kinds of sin that destroy God's creation. The ecclesiology of prophetic participation invites the faith community to go back to the life of Jesus who lived out the faith to correct the systems and to affirm life. As a visible body of Jesus, the Church has to condemn all forms of sin. It should fight against injustice in socio-political realms and reclaim justice. The issues faced by people should be the focus of the Church's participation in the mission of Jesus Christ.

The ecclesiology of M. M. Thomas criticises evil tendencies inside and outside the Church and interprets Gospel for a new society, which is based on the values of New Humanity in Christ. It seeks the relevance of Christian faith in historical situations in which people encounter injustice, human rights violations, casteism, degradation of human values and dignity. It upholds that salvation and humanisation are integrally related and rejects evangelical tendency to limit the Christian mission to preaching and church growth. Christianity is true humanism having power to transform world communities in relation to freedom, justice and love.

The concept of New Humanity in Christ is the subject of an important theological discussion of M. M. Thomas. He related this with the mission of the Church in contemporary society. For him, the Church is the sign and sacrament of New Humanity, which is given by God in Jesus Christ. It can be considered as a fellowship that transcends all divisions based on religion, race, nation, class, sex, caste, etc., and endorses humanisation and oneness in Christ. This concept has multi-dimensional applications and covers all aspects of human life. Jesus is the source of the New Humanity that is characterised by the experience of liberating faith and liberating grace, which transcends the borders of the visible church.

New Humanity offers liberation from all kinds of oppression and envisages a new cosmos. It transforms all world communities and abolishes the walls of religious exclusiveness. It stands for the renewal and ultimate humanisation of society. The Church is the prophetic sign of New Humanity, which stands for a richer human life. So, the divine commission of the Church is to witness the Gospel of New Humanity, which renews the entire humanity in Christ. Christ, the source of New Humanity, brings renewal to the inner being of humans, human relations and the cosmos. Since New Humanity is concerned with active participation in the struggles for a new human society, it gets involved in the pertinent issues of contemporary society. It discerns Christ in the struggles of people who are deprived of justice, freedom, equality, dignity, etc. It is an instrument of transformation and aims at an egalitarian society that upholds the values of Kingdom of God.

The Church is the sign and sacrament of New Humanity, which is called to respond to the social realities of respective locations. But the Church often fails to accomplish the mission of New Humanity in Christ. Injustice and inequality disfigure the fabric of our society. The gap between the rich and the poor is ever widening. Privatisation of resources and the exploitative approach of multinational companies causes poverty and unemployment among ordinary unskilled people. The dominant groups in society enslave marginalised groups such as the dalits and the tribals. In fact, they are thrown out of the mainstream of society. People are categorised on the basis of money and mode of consumption in society. In this context, the Church is called to witness the message of New Humanity, which advocates the values of social justice and human dignity. The Church should participate in the struggles of the poor for social justice and human rights in the society. The Church must chalk out programmes for the upliftment of those who are deprived of equal rights and dignity. In order to accomplish its social mission, the Church as a sign of New Humanity should encourage social action groups and take part in their programmes against unjust activities and violence of the dominant sections of society. Since in Christ there is no discrimination based on sex, race, caste and class, it is the duty of the Church to conscientise people against communal and caste feelings. As a New Humanity in Christ, the Christian community is called to protect the basic rights of all people and to become prophetic witness in the context of dehumanisation, cultural disintegration and degeneration of kingdom values such as justice, equality, righteousness, freedom, peace and love.

The concept of New Humanity promotes the active participation of the Church in political struggles for just cause. In the context of corruption and human rights violation, the Church's political mission is the eradication of corruption and injustice in the world of politics. The Church's political involvement is not for communal interests but for the interests of common people. The Church as the sign of New Humanity is for the humanisation of the entire humanity. So, the Church cannot remain silent about issues such as systematic violence and gender discrimination. The Church is responsible for giving ideological and moral support to the political movements of the dalits and the tribals who fight against the negation of their rights and privileges. What we need today is an ecclesiastical structure that raises voice against corruptibility of power and unjust political motives of political parties and communities. Since, New Humanity stands for the welfare of all, the Church should conscientise the unfortunate illiterate people about their political rights and privileges. The Church must leave the non-political approach and involve itself in the political process for humanisation and just society.

New Humanity in Christ transcends all religious exclusiveness and encourages secular human fellowship for the development of human society. It envisages the renewal of humanity and ideologies since Christ is abolishing or at least lowering the walls of religious barriers and ethos. As the sign of New Humanity, the Church's mission in the pluralistic context is to discern God's renewing work even outside the Church. So, the Church should enter into inter-faith dialogue and inter-faith relations for responding to common human challenges, such as religious disharmony, fundamentalism and communal conflicts. As a source of renewal and new creation, the Church should be an inclusive community that accepts all groups of people with the love of God. In a context where different religions and ideologies co-exist, the mission of the Church is to convey the message of love, peace, harmony and reconciliation. The Church as a witnessing community of New Humanity is responsible for working for communal unity through dialogue. Dialogue can solve communal tensions among religions. In short, the Church should join with people of other faiths for a richer expression of human life and for ushering in true humanism, which transcends all divisions.

The Church symbolises the New Humanity in Christ, which is characterised by forgiveness, genuine fellowship, reconciliation and unity. It renews the Church completely. But today's Church is gripped by divisions, discrimination, disunity, etc. As a sign of New Humanity in Christ, the Church is based on fellowship in Christ, which defends the values of justice and equality. In the midst of gender discrimination, the gap between the rich and the poor, the caste system, etc., the mission of the Church is to bring people into fellowship in Christ. The purpose of the New Humanity in Christ is to bring transformation in the ecclesiastical setup and in various spheres of human life. The Church, as an agent of transformation and a model community, has to challenge what is evil in the world.

The New Humanity in Christ has a message of the renewal of all things in the world. God renews and thus makes all things new; He gives a new human nature, a new humanity and a new cosmos. The purpose of this renewal is to prevent the world from degradation and perversion. The Church is not just a religious institution but people acknowledging God's renewal of all things in Christ. The ecological mission of the Church is to protect nature from all kinds of exploitation and to renew the whole cosmos. The Church, the sign of New Humanity, should understand that both eco-justice and social justice are integrally related. Since New Humanity is for the protection and renewal of the whole cosmos, the Church is called to respond to the ecological crisis caused by the existing capitalist and lopsided development. Very often, the Church fails to respond meaningfully to natural exploitation and deforestation. In the context of ecological issues, the Church should conscientise people on the importance of protecting nature and resisting the exploitative outlook of multinational companies.

New Humanity offers a richer and fuller human life, and it is the role of the Church to express its solidarity with those who search for fuller human life, especially the dalits and the tribals. It calls for solidarity with the oppressed and exhorts others to help the poor in their struggles of liberation from all kinds of socio-religious and political disabilities. Instead of following a non-political approach, the Church should support them in their struggle for social justice.

The ecclesiology of Paulose Mar Paulose reminds us that the Church is an important tool in God's revolutionary strategy and that the political witness of the Church is to participate in the struggles and life-realities of people, particularly those who are outside the faith community. The Church has to activate its faith to serve people irrespective of their religious affiliations. It calls the faith community to help those who are powerless and voiceless in establishing their rights and privileges. Political witness is an effective means of witness in society. The political responsibility of the Church involves a constructive and critical relationship with the State. Therefore, the exclusive understanding of political witness must be transformed into creative societal engagement with a sense of responsibility.

The Ecclesiology of Mar Paulose teaches the present Church that the God whom we meet in the Bible can be understood only in relation to the freedom of people from the clutches of oppressive structures. Jesus reveals that God is a revolutionary being who always identified with human struggles. Therefore, Christian spirituality is for struggle and for resisting the evil forces in society. The role of religion in society and politics is transformative and prophetic. The Church as the community of God has only one mission, i.e.

struggle for justice. The political witness of the Church is not meant for protecting rights and privileges, but to engage with the life-realities of people. It also challenges the Church to understand minority rights in the light of human rights. The ecumenical movements in India should be encouraged to respond to the hopes and aspirations of the marginalised. As a community responsive to human values, the Church in a multi-faith context is accountable to protect the fundamental rights of all citizens in a secular society. The communal identity of the Church can be changed by participating in the socio-political-economic struggles for justice.

The ecclesiology of Paulose Mar Paulose affirms that political witness is for the welfare of society. It is a theological praxis that discovers God in the life of poor people and leads them to celebration of life. Political witness challenges the Church to have solidarity with the people who are alienated from the mainstream. Therefore, spirituality should be re-interpreted for political witness. The Church's political engagement must be of liberative politics, not of communal politics. Since political witness affirms life, it can be better considered as a sacramental act. As it upholds the values of God's kingdom, political witness can be regarded as a foretaste of the Reign of God. Political witness stimulates the Church to claim that the Church is not a communal entity but Jesus community. In order to respond to the issues faced by subaltern people, the Church must be a community of subaltern consciousness. In short, the Church in a pluralistic context cannot be a communal organisation. Its political witness is to safeguard the life of the entire humanity. Indeed, the Church exists for prophetic participation.

Bibliography

Books

Athyal, M. Yesudas. ed. M.M. Thomas, *The Man and His Legacy*. Manjadi: The Thiruvalla Ecumenical Charitable Trust and Thiruvalla: CSS, 1997.

Augustine, Saint. *The City of God*. New York: Image Books Double Day, 1958.

Barnhill, Carla. *A Year with Dietrich Bonhoeffer*. New York: HarperCollins, 2005.

Bhasin, Kamla. *What is Patriarchy?* New Delhi: Kali for Women, 1993.

Boff, Leonardo. *Church: Charism and Power*. New York: The Cross Road Publishing Company, 1988.

Bonhoeffer, Dietrich. *The Cost of Discipleship*. London: SCM Press Ltd, 1959.

Bonhoeffer, Dietrich. *Ethics*. New York: Mac Millan Company, 1962.

Bonhoeffer, Dietrich. *No Rusty Swords*. New York: Harper & Row Publishers, 1965.

Bonhoeffer, Dietrich. *Christology*. London: Collins, 1966.

Bonhoeffer, Dietrich. *Letters and Papers from Prison*. New York: Macmillan Publishing, 1972.

Bibliography

Bonhoeffer, Dietrich. *A Testament to Freedom: The Essential Writings of Dietrich Bonhoeffer*. San Francisco: Harper- Sanfrancisco, 1995.

Bonhoeffer, Dietrich. *Ethics*. Minneapolis: Fortress Press, 2005.

Bosanquent, Mary. *The Life and Death of Dietrich Bonhoeffer*. London: Hodder and Stoughton, 1968.

Boyd, Robin. *An Introduction to Indian Christian Theology*. Delhi: ISPCK, 2005.

Coward, Harold. *Pluralism in the World Religions*. Oxford : One World Publications, 2000.

Desrochers, John. *Towards a New India*. Bangalore: CSA, 1995.

Desrochers, John. *The Social Teaching of the Church in India*. Bangalore: NBCLC/CSA, 2006.

Dietrich, Gabriele and Bas Wielenga. *Towards Understanding Indian Society*. Madurai: TTS, 1997.

Ebeling, Gerhard. *Luther, An Introduction to His Thought*. Philadelphia: Fortress Press, 1980.

Godsey, John D. *The Theology of Dietrich Bonhoeffer*. London: SCM Press Ltd, 1960.

Grenz, Stanly J. and Roger E. Olson, *20th Century Theology*. Secunderabad: OM Books, 1992.

John Hall, Douglas. *Remembered Voices*. Louisville: West minister John Knox Press, 1998.

Kappen, S. *Jesus and Society*. Delhi: ISPCK, 2002.

Koshy, Ninan. *Caste in the Kerala Churches*. Bangalore: CISRS, 1968.

Moltmann, Jurgen. *Theology of Hope*. London: SCM Press Ltd, 1967.

Paulose, Paulose Mar. *Church's* Mission. Bombay: BUILD, n.d.

Paulose, Paulose Mar. *Swathanthryamanu Daivam* (Malayalam).Ariyannur: Patabhedam, 1996.

Paulose, Paulose Mar. *Nisabdharayirikkan Ningalkkenthadhikaram?* (Malayalam). Noorannad: Fabian Books, 1998.

Paulose, Paulose Mar. *Spirituality for Struggle*. Thiruvalla: CSS, 1999.

Paulose, Paulose Mar. *Dhaivathe Charithrathilekku Thurannu Viduka* (Malayalam). Thrissur: Bishop Paulose Mar Paulose Foundation for Socio-Cultural Development, 2000.

Paulose, Paulose Mar. *Encounter in Humanization*.Tiruvalla: CSS, 2000.

Paulose, Paulose Mar. *Vithakyappetta Vithukal* (Malayalam) Collection by K.J Thomas. Thrissur: Poulose Mar Poulose Foundation for Social Development, 2005.

Philip, T.M. *The Encounter Between Theology and Ideology: An Exploration into the Communicative Theology of M.M. Thomas*. Madras: The CLS, 1986.

Rasmussen, Larry L. *Dietrich Bonhoeffer, Reality and Resistance*. Louisville: Westminster John Knox Press, 2005.

Rao, Amruta. *Sex Discrimination*. Delhi: Indian Publishers Distributors, 2000.

Roark, Dallas M. *Dietrich Bonhoeffer*. London: Word Books, 1975.

Russel, Letty M. *Church in the Round*. Louisville: Westminister/John Knox Press, 1993.

Stephen, M. *A Christian Theology in the Indian Context*. Delhi: ISPCK, 2001.

Thomas, M.M. *Salvation and Humanization*. Madras: The CLS, 1971.

_____., *Christava Samuhia Dharmam* [Mal.]. Thiruvalla: The TLC, 1972.

_____., *Man and the Universe of Faiths*. Madras: CISRS-CLS, 1975.

_____., *New Creation in Christ*. Delhi : ISPCK, 1976.

_____., *The Secular Ideologies of India and the Secular Meaning of Christ*. Madras : The CLS for CISRS, Bangalore, 1976.

_____., *Sarva Srushtikkum Aadya Jathan* [Mal.]. Thiruvalla : The CLS, 1977.

_____., *Aadiyil Daivam* [Mal.]. Thiruvalla : The CLS, 1977.

_____., *Some Theological Dialogues*. Madras : The CLS, 1977.

Bibliography

_____., *Towards a Theology of Contemporary Ecumenism*. Madras : The CLS, 1978.

_____., *Revolution in India and Christian Humanism*. Delhi: Forum for Christian Concern for People's Struggle, 1978.

_____., *Response to Tyranny*. Delhi: Forum for Christian Concern for People's Struggle, 1979.

_____., *Theekshnathaulla Daivam* [Mal.]. Thiruvalla : The CLS, 1979.

_____., *Yesuvil Daivarajyam Sameepam* [Mal.]. Thiruvalla : The CLS, 1981.

_____., *Religion and the Revolt of the Oppressed*. Delhi : ISPCK, 1981.

_____., *Parivarthanathinte Daivasasthram* [Mal.]. Thiruvalla : The TLC, 1982.

_____., *Yesu Christuvil Oru Puthiya Manushian* [Mal.] Thiruvalla : The CLS, 1983.

_____., *Ideological Quest within Christian Commitment 1939-54*. Madras : The CLS for CISRS, Bangalore, 1983.

_____., *Church and Human Community*. Delhi : ISPCK, 1985.

_____., *Bharathathil Christava Sabhayude Samuhika Dharmam* [Mal.]. Thiruvalla : The TLC, 1985.

_____., *Vimochakanaya Daivam* (Mal.). Thiruvalla : The CLS, 1985.

_____., *Recalling Ecumenical Beginnings*. Delhi : ISPCK, 1987.

_____., *Risking Christ for Christ's Sake : Towards an Ecumenical Theology of Pluralism*. Geneva : WCC Publications, 1987.

_____., *Faith and Ideology in the Struggle for Justice*. Bombay : BUILD, 1987.

_____., *Faith, Communality and Community*. Thiruvalla : PSA, 1987.

_____., *My Ecumenical Journey*. Trivandrum : P.M. Oommen of Ecumenical Publishing Centre, 1990.

_____., *The Acknowledged Christ of the Indian Renaissance.* Madras : The CLS, 1991.

_____., *The Nagas Towards AD 2000.* Madras: Centre for Research on New International Economic Order, 1992.

_____., *The Gospel of Forgiveness and Koinonia.* Delhi: ISPCK and Thiruvalla: CSS, 1994.

_____., *A Diaconal Approach to Indian Ecclesiology.* Rome: CIIS and Thiruvalla: CSS, 1995.

_____., *The Church's Mission and Post Modern Humanism.* Delhi: ISPCK and Thiruvalla: CSS, 1996.

Thomas, M.M. and P.T. Thomas. *Towards an Indian Christian Theology, Life and Thought of Some Pioneers.* Thiruvalla: The New Day Publications of India, 1992.

Thomas, T. Jacob. ed. *M.M. Thomas Reader, Selected Texts on Theology, Religion and Society.* Thiruvalla : CSS, 2002.

Vargheese, E.T, ed. *Appam, Samathum, Swathathrym* (Malayalam).Thrissur: Bishop Paulose Mar Paulose Foundation for Socio-Cultural Development, 2000.

Wolters, T. Hielke. *Theology of Prophetic Participation, M.M. Thomas' Concept of Salvation and the Collective Struggle for Fuller Humanity in India.* Delhi: ISPCK and Bangalore: UTC, 1996.

Human Rights Watch. *Broken People, Caste Violence Against India's "Untouchables"* New York: Human Rights Watch, 1999.

Works of Martin Luther Vol. IV. Philadelphia: Muhlenberg Press, 1931.

Articles in Books

Devasahayam, V. "Search for the Last, the Least and the Lost – Dr. M.M. Thomas' Understanding of the Humans, God and the New Humanity." In *Christian Witness in society.* Edited by K.C. Abraham. Bangalore: BTE-SSC, 1998.

Leibholz, G. "Memoir." In Dietrich Bonhoeffer, *The Cost of Discipleship* (Bombay: St.Paul Publications, (Indian Edition) 1974.

Leith, John H. "Ecclesiology." In *A New Hand Book of Christian Theology.* Edited by Donald W. Musser and Joseph L. Prince. Nashville: Abingdon Press, 1992.

Marsh, Charles. "Dietrich Bonhoeffer." In *The Modern Theologians*. Edited by David F. Ford. Oxford: Blackwell Publishers, 1997.

Scott, C. David. "A Mirror to M.M. Thomas' Perspective on Inter-Religious Studies." In *Christian Witness in Society*. Edited by K.C. Abraham. Bangalore: BTE-SCC, 1998.

Thomas, MM. "Christian Insights for Politics." In *Political Outlook in India Today*. Edited by J.R. Chandran and M.M. Thomas. Bangalore: Committee for Literature on Social Concerns, 1956.

_____., "Search for a New Humanism as Foundation for the Struggle for a Just Society." In *Political Prospects in India*. Edited by Saral K. Chatterji. Madras: The CLS, 1971.

_____. "A Spirituality for Combat." In *Freedom Love Community*. Edited by K.M. George. Madras: The CLS, 1985.

_____., "Christian Social Thought and Action – A Necessary Tragedy." In *Christian Ethics – An Introductory Reader*. Edited by Hunter P. Mabry. Calcutta: ITL-SSC, 1987.

_____., "The Use and Place of the Bible for Christians in their Professional and Social Involvement." In *The Bible in Today's Context*. Edited by S. Immanuel David. Calcutta: BTE-SSC, 1987.

_____., "The Secular Ideologies of India and the Secular Meaning of Christ." In *Readings in Indian Christian Theology* Vol.I. Edited by R.S. Sugirtharajah and Cecil Hargreaves. Delhi: ISPCK, 1993.

_____., The Church – The Fellowship of the Baptized and the Unbaptized." In *Liberating Witness*. Edited by Prasanna Kumari. Madras: The Gurukul Lutheran Theological College and Research Institute, 1995.

_____., "The Cultural Mission of Catholic Education in Nagaland." In *Culture, Religion and Society*. Edited by Saral K. Chatterji and Hunter P. Mabry. Delhi: ISPCK, 1996.

_____., "Criteria of a Living Theology." In *Asian Expressions of Christian Commitment, A Reader in Asian Theology*. Edited by T.Dayanandan Francis and F.J. Balasundaram. Madras: The CLS, 1996.

Thomas, T. Jacob. "Insights from M.M. Thomas for an Ethical Christology." In *Christian Witness in Society*. Edited by K.C. Abraham. Bangalore: BTE-SCC, 1998.

Articles in Journals and Periodicals

Chandra Jena, Purna. "Bloody Christmas-2007." *People's Reporter* Vol. 21/ No.1 (January 10-25, 2008): 4&6.

"Christians and the Emergency: Some Documents," *Religion and Society* Vol. XXIV/ No. 2&3 (June-September, 1977).

Dabhi, Jimmy. "Dalit Human Rights: Issues and Perspective." *Social Action* Vol. 54/No.1 (January-March, 2004): 33-46.

David, James. "Special Economic Zones." *Integral Liberation* Vol. 2/ No. 3 (September, 2007): 182-194.

D'souza, Simon Paul. "India At Sixty." *Integral Liberation* Vol. 2/No.3 (September, 2007): 171-181.

Editorial, "Sukhdeo Thorat Committee Report: Caste Discrimination in AIIMS." *Economic and Political Weekly* Vol. XLII/No.22 (June 2-8, 2007): 2031-2033.

Hemrom, A.S. "Role of Churches towards building up Adivasi Solidarity: The Call for an Ecumenical Task." *NCC Review* Vol. CXXIV/No. 2 (February, 2004): 63-72.

John, T.A. "Gender Equality: Chasing a Millennium Goal for the Long Haul." *Social Action* Vol. 57/No.2 (April-June, 2007): 160-170.

Lobo, Lancy. "Communalism and Christian Response in India." *Vidyajyoti Journal of Theological Reflections* Vol.LIX/No.6 (June, 1995): 365-374.

Massey, James. "An Analysis of the Dalit situation with Special Reference to Dalit Christians and Dalit Theology." *Religion and Society* Vol. 52/No. 3-4 (September- December, 2007): 57-86.

Mitra, N.B. "Bishops Condemn Govt. Assault on Minority Rights." *People's Reporter* Vol. 20/No.3 (February 10-25, 2007): 3.

Moses, Y. "Peoples' Politics and the Role of the Indian Church." *NCC Review* Vol. CXXVI/No.10 (November, 2006): 49-52.

Paulose, Paulose Mar. "Indian Christian Theology, the Church and the People." *Religion and Society* Vol.XXX / No 384 (September-December, 1983): 87-91.

Puniyani, Ram. "Common Minimum Programme and Outcome for Secularism." *Social Action* Vol. 56/No.3 (July-September, 2006):289-294.

Radha Krishnan, M.G. "Ire of the Minorities." *India Today* Vol. XXXIII/No. 1 (January 1-7, 2008): 20-21.

Rochelle, Jay C. "Bonhoeffer: Community, Authority and Spirituality." *Currents in Theology and Mission* Vol. 21/No.2 (April, 1994), 117-122.

Sahoo, Sarbeswar. "Tribal Displacement and Human Rights Violations in Orissa." *Social Action* Vol. 55/No. 2 (April-June, 2005): 153-165.

Smith, G.R. "The Ecclesiology of M.M. Thomas." *The SATHRI Journal* No.2 (1993): 34-50.

Thomas, M.M. "Spirituality for Combat." *NCC Review* Vol. CXVI/No.1 (1996): 33-55.

_____., "A Rewarding Correspondence with the Late Dr. Hendrik Kraemer." *Religion and Society* Vol. 13 (June, 1966): 5-11.

_____. , "Theological aspects of the Relationship between Social Action Groups and Churches." *Religion and Society* Vol. XXXI/No.2 (June, 1984): 19-36.

_____., "The Churches and the Future of Indian Democracy." *NCCR* Vol. XCVII/6-7 (June-July, 1977): 341-344.

_____., "Promotion of World Development Services and the Problem of Relationships." *Religion and Society* Vol. 19/No.3 (1972): 35-46.

Thomas, K.T. "Not an Article of Special Privilege but Only a Provision for Protection." Reported by Rev. Dr. R.C.Thomas, *People's Reporter* Vol. 19/No.14 (July 25 – August 10, 2006): 1&7.

Weizsacker, Carl Friedrich von. "Thoughts of a Non-Theologian on Dietrich Bonhoeffer's Theological Development." *The Ecumenical Review* Vol.28/No.2 (April, 1976): 156-165.

Wilfred, Felix. "Subalterns and Ethical Auditing." *Jeevadhara* Vol. XXXVII/No.217 (January, 2007): 5-23.

Zachariah, George. "The Grand Inquisitor and the Syrian Christian Primates in Kerala: Musings on the Pastoral Letter." *Gurukul Journal of Theological Studies* Vol. XVIII/ No.1 (January, 2007): 40-48.

Article in Dictionary

Mcbrien, Richard P. "Church." *A New Dictionary of Christian Theology*. Edited by Alan Richardson and John Bowden. London: SCM Press Ltd, 1983, 108-110.

Unpublished Thesis

DeenaBandhu, Manchala. *"Towards a Dalit Ecclesiology An Examination of the Writings of Select Dalit Theologians."* M.Th. Thesis, Senate of Serampore College, 1994.

Movie

Bonhoeffer, Agent of Grace. Winner of Best Film at Monte Carlo Television Festival, 2000.

Interview

Koshy, Ninan. Social Activist in Trivandrum. Interview, 24 April 2007.

Webliography

Britannica, Encyclopedia. "Adolf von Harnack." *http://www.britannica.com/eb/article- 9001567/Adolf-von-Harnack*, (7 September 2007).

Laughlin, Matt Mc. "Dietrich Bonhoeffer." *httt://people.bu.edu. /wwildman/Weird Wild Web/courses/mwt/dictionary/mut-themes-780-bonhoeffer.htm* (7 September 2007).

www.ingramcontent.com/pod-product-compliance
Lightning Source LLC
Chambersburg PA
CBHW031955080426
42735CB00007B/401